Fairways and Greens

Also by Dan Jenkins

Bubba Talks
You Gotta Play Hurt
"You Call It Sports But I Say It's a Jungle
   Out There"
Fast Copy
Football (*with Walter Iooss, Jr.*)
Life Its Ownself
Baja Oklahoma
Limo (*with Bud Shrake*)
Dead Solid Perfect
Semi-Tough
Saturday's America
The Dogged Victims of Inexorable Fate
The Best 18 Golf Holes in America

DAN JENKINS

Fairways and Greens

The Best Golf Writing of Dan Jenkins

DOUBLEDAY

New York   London   Toronto   Sydney   Auckland

PUBLISHED BY DOUBLEDAY
a division of Bantam Doubleday Dell Publishing Group, Inc.
1540 Broadway, New York, New York 10036

DOUBLEDAY and the portrayal of an anchor with a dolphin
are trademarks of Doubleday, a division of
Bantam Doubleday Dell Publishing Group, Inc.

Articles appearing herein have previously apeared in *Golf Digest.*

Library of Congress Cataloging-in-Publication Data

Jenkins, Dan.
Fairways and greens: the best golf writing of Dan Jenkins.—1st ed.
p. cm.
1. Golf—Anecdotes.   I. Title.
GV967.J417   1994
796.352—dc20   93-45464
CIP

ISBN 0-385-47425-3

This book is dedicated to a foursome:

for Bud Shrake, who has come to love golf more than writing, or even tunafish;

for Dave Marr, who has never let golf interfere with laughter;

for Don Matheson, another old friend who has always been there;

and for Jerry Tarde, as fine an editor as ever lifted a sentence out of a bunker and gave it a better lie.

Contents

FOREWORD   ix

PREFACE   xi

PART ONE   The Way It Is Today—Dining Out
on Corporate Logos

The Best Things in Golf   3
The Host Club   9
Designers and Developers   13
"He's Safely On"   17
Bobby Joe Grooves   21
What If the Tour Stopped Tomorrow?   24
Tour Pro Seeks New Line of Work   28
Media Messages   32
The Man Himself   35
Be Happy with Second Place   38

Saving the World   43

The World of Golf on Cable TV   47

Things That Make You Hot   50

Golf Nuts   54

Riding High   58

The Luck of Calcutta Bob and Suntan Jim   62

Debunking the Firm Left Side   65

What Is This Lost-Ball Business?   69

The Perfect Driver   73

Hap McWedge and the Senior Amateurs   77

The Most Dangerous Job in Golf   81

PART TWO   Order the Nostalgia and Tell Them
Heavy on the Hogan

Hogan   87

The Mother of All Streaks   104

Old Tom   109

The Towering Inferno   115

The Masters Its Ownself   121

Back to Baltus Oak   132

Whoo-Ha, Arnie!   138

The Dream Tournament   149

The Glory Game at Goat Hills   163

A Semi-Tough Return to Golf   180

Golf with the Boss   198

"You'll Not Do That Here, Laddie"   216

AFTERWORD   244

Foreword

WHEN WORD began to circulate through pro shops, grillrooms, and various dark alleys that this collection was going to be brought out—well, you can imagine how chaotic things got around the house.

My twenty-four-hour Golfline was overwhelmed, for one thing. This is a counseling service that is normally subscribed to by people who want to be cured of talking about handicap indexes, the spin rate of square grooves, and the modified Stableford scoring system.

I must have received at least four calls from lovers of the game who begged me not to forget to include some of their old favorites. These were stories they thought they remembered reading in magazines once upon a time, although they weren't entirely certain about the byline.

If the callers were in fact talking about my work, they were kind enough not to mention that the pieces had found an even greater usefulness around their homes in lining kitchen shelves for cans of pinto beans and jars of mustard.

The bulk of this stuff *has* appeared in magazines before, of course, in *Golf Digest* and *Sports Illustrated,* the two campuses where I have spent the past three decades lecturing to innocent bystanders and pretending to work for a living.

A few of the efforts have even sneaked into anthologies over the years, as I'm sure you are aware of if you follow all of the urban disturbances caused by the frantic book-buying public where anthologies are concerned.

But there is quite a bit of fresh material here, either in the form of essays or what I would call a combination of transplants and face-lifts.

One of the pleasures of putting together a collection, I think, is being able to tamper with the old prose. You are occasionally inclined to scratch out or rewrite whole sentences, if not whole paragraphs. This is after you have slapped yourself around like one of the Three Stooges, and shouted, "Jesus God, what idiot could have written that?"

This book takes its title from a good many golfers I know who say "Fairways and greens" to friends the way other people say "Drive carefully" or "Have a good life."

"Fairways and greens," the way I generally use it, means I hope you make it through the day without getting hurt.

As for the name of the writer that appears in the subtitle, I can only remark on what an incredible coincidence it is.

D.J.

Preface

JACK NICKLAUS, comma.

That's the line that would stay with most of us the longest, the thing that was most often said over a period of, oh, twenty-five years, I guess.

All it took was for Nicklaus to go up on the leader board. It didn't matter what round it was. It didn't matter how many strokes behind he might be. It didn't matter how many brand names were ahead of him. Somebody in the pressroom would say it.

"Want some coffee?"

"Jack Nicklaus, comma."

"Yep. Cream and sugar?"

A whole quarter-century of my joyride in covering golf tournaments seemed to run parallel with Nicklaus winning golf tournaments.

I should mention that this was nothing to complain about. Not if you liked seeing your copy get good play.

The difference between Nicklaus winning a golf

tournament, particularly a major championship, and a mere mortal winning a golf tournament—God forbid a major—was, like, huge.

For a newspaper slave, it could make the difference between a six-column headline and a two-column head. For a magazine servant, it could make the difference between a cover story and a spot in the back of the book with ice fishing.

So it goes in journalism, which doesn't make the news, it only delivers it to a readership that loves to fondle celebrities.

In golf, this has never made the mere mortals happy. But the truth is, it has always made editors happy back in the office, editors by and large being a subnormal form of human life, people who seldom get to go to the Monterey Peninsula or St. Andrews as often as golf writers do.

It's an astonishing thing, but I sometimes found myself being congratulated for a job well done by a boss of one kind or another in my *Sports Illustrated* days when Nicklaus pulled out a victory in a major, something like a Masters. It was as if I had been personally responsible for saving the publication that week.

At the same time, I could catch a share of the blame if I had been careless enough to allow a mere mortal to win, a fellow along the lines of a George Archer, a Dave Stockton, or a Lou Graham.

"How could you have let that happen?" an editor back in the office would say, rather coolly, and only half-joking.

Which reminds me of the time I made a bad joke in print about George Archer. I said something like he would still come up short on charisma if he happened to be riding in a golf cart with Jill St. John. Something brilliantly tasteless like that.

A week or so later, I received a testy letter from Mrs. George Archer, who said, among other things, "I will have you know that my husband has more charisma than Joe Namath and Gary Cooper combined!"

While I was amused to see those two names lumped together in the same context, I left the response up to a cynical cohort in the pressroom. He read that part of the letter, and said, "She's right—Namath's got a busted knee and Gary Cooper's dead!"

There was this occasion when I strongly suggested in print that Arnold Palmer should have won the PGA Championship in 1970 at Southern Hills in Tulsa instead of Dave Stockton, who was then a member of the tour's invisible rank and file.

I wasn't the only writer who thought Palmer had played the best golf that week and Stockton had played the luckiest golf that week, but I was the guy who wrote it in *Sports Illustrated,* which had color pictures, and that evidently compounded the crime, as Stockton saw it.

Stockton didn't understand or appreciate that angling the piece around Arnold focused ever more attention on him, the winner.

But no matter. A few weeks later, the responsibility of defending me fell upon Bob Drum, an old pressroom compatriot. Legend has it that during a tournament in New Jersey, Stockton went up to Drum and in a rather fierce tone of voice said, "Is Jenkins here? I want to *talk* to him!"

Calmly, Drum said, "I don't think he's coming this week. Whom shall I say is asking?"

One of my favorite moments involving mere mortals occurred in 1975 at the U.S. Open at Medinah outside of Chicago, where Lou Graham and John Mahaffey wound up in an 18-hole playoff.

The fact that I would be forced to stay over another day did not annoy me. I am proud to say that I am not one of those poets who gripe about 18-hole playoffs. I think all majors are too important to be settled at sudden death, and it saddens me that the Masters, British Open, and PGA have all caved in to the wishes of network television, which cares a lot less about golf's traditions than it does about the commercials in daytime soap operas.

Anyhow, Lou Graham won the playoff at Medinah and now I'm on a furious Monday deadline, and I'm trying to work in the usual slum of a USGA press tent. It's boiling hot, the workspace is cramped, and there aren't even any soft drinks available anymore. "Unions don't do playoffs," some guy explained.

Suddenly, someone tapped on my shoulder. "What?" I snarled, wheeling around, looking no more irritated than a man with a boot on his chest.

It was Patsy Graham, Lou's wife. And in a soft Southern accent, smiling sweetly, she said, "Be nice, Dan. He's really a good guy."

I could only laugh, and I'm certain that whatever I wrote was a little nicer than it might have been ordinarily.

The comma thing didn't start with Nicklaus, incidentally.

Before Jack came along, we said, "Arnold Palmer, comma," and before Arnold came along, we said, "Ben Hogan, comma."

In the era of Hogan, and purely for the amusement of it, we also spoke in the clichés that were a legacy of bygone writers.

"I see where Slammin' Sam Snead, the West Virginia hillbilly, has a one-stroke lead on Dr. Cary Middlecoff, the golfing dentist," somebody would mention.

A reply might be, "Yes, but I wouldn't count out Mustachioed Lloyd Magnum, the riverboat gambler, or Colorful Jimmy Demaret, golf's goodwill ambassador."

To which a third party would remark, "I rather fancy Bantam Ben Hogan, the Wee leemon, myself, or perhaps Lord Byron Nelson, golf's mechanical man."

Today, the comma thing can often work in reverse for the pressroom cynics. Let's say you have a leader board that is momentarily populated with marquee names like Greg Norman, Nick Price, Nick Faldo, Tom Kite, and Curtis Strange, but there happens to be one lurker among them. A Greg Twiggs, for instance, just to grab a name at random.

Naturally, you know what to expect. More than one fellow writer, sensing doom, fearing the worst, will stroll past you and quietly murmur, "Greg Twiggs, comma."

Believe it. Writers don't root for people, they root for stories.

Somebody once said it's hard to care about a sport that doesn't have a literature. Golf certainly has a literature, I'm happy to say, as do football, baseball, boxing, and horse racing, to name the only others that come immediately to mind, but go ahead and care about tennis and basketball if you must.

In my younger days of clacking on the typewriter in press tents, the older gentlemen who were covering golf at the time wore coats and ties and approached the game with the fervor of a religious zealot who also felt an urgent calling to become a landscape artist. They would ignore a competitor's quotes, regardless of how colorfully he might speak, preferring instead to hold their readers captive in Augusta's "cathedral of pines."

I myself always thought it was as much fun to listen to golf as it was to watch it, possibly because I spent so many years gambling on public courses with a splendid variety of thieves and vagrants.

My typewriter never needed an outfielder's glove to reach up and catch the phrase the first time it heard a competitor say he had to "steer-job" his tee ball at the second, or he had to "cold-jump a 2-iron" to reach the fifth, or he "overpured" his 5-iron at the twelfth, or he "three-jacked it" on the seventeenth green.

Unless you're a dues-paying member of the press-room's point-missers, you know these expressions have instantly entered the lexicon.

Speaking of point-missers, if I don't steer-job this back to Jack Nicklaus, I think I'm going to find myself among them.

It was always easy to be nice to Nicklaus in print, of course—even before he trimmed down, fluff-dried his hair, and stopped looking like an offensive tackle who had escaped the grasp of Woody Hayes. It was Nicklaus, after all, who changed the game. Ushered in a new dawn, as they say—comma.

Other engagingly long hitters had come along before Jack—Jimmy Thomson and George Bayer having achieved the most fame for it—but there had never been a player as consistently long *and* straight as Nicklaus.

When this beefy kid with a crew cut out of Columbus, Ohio, had the audacity to beat Arnold Palmer in that playoff for the 1962 U.S. Open at Oakmont, and do it essentially by outdriving Palmer by about 50 yards on every long hole, you could only gape at what was happening and utter something on the order of, "Dear me, what have we here?"

Of all the thrilling moments Jack provided for us— like three decades' worth, if you're scoring—I seem to remember a select few of them more vividly than all of the others.

No eyewitness could ever forget Nicklaus on the eighteenth hole at St. Andrews in the playoff with Doug Sanders for the 1970 British Open. Sanders had trailed by four strokes with five holes to play, but somehow he made up three shots through the seventeenth. He was only one back when he drove exquisitely off the eighteenth tee, putting himself in shape for a little bump-and-run shot up to the flag for a birdie that might tie and force a sudden-death thing.

Nicklaus saw that he needed a birdie three to cinch victory. Obviously, he needed to make something happen. Jack intensified the drama by slipping out of his cardigan before addressing the tee shot, and he seemed to take an abnormal amount of time to consider the tight boundary on the right. Then he smashed a howling monster, a drive of 370 yards that carried over the crosswalk and burned its way through the Valley of Sin and didn't stop until it was on the back fringe of the green. From there, he got down in two for the birdie that won it for him.

When Jack reflects back on that drama these days, he likes to grin and say, "A driver was too much club," but between you and me, I think he relishes that moment, too.

I remember the shot at Augusta in 1975 that for much of its flight looked like a double eagle without knickers.

This was Jack's 1-iron second shot to the fifteenth in

the final round of the Masters on Sunday afternoon when he was trying to catch and beat Johnny Miller and Tom Weiskopf—and did.

One stroke behind with four holes left to play, it was again time for Nicklaus to "make something happen." In the middle of the fifteenth fairway, he knew he had exactly 240 yards to the flag, but more important, he knew he had 220 yards to carry the ever-dangerous blue pond in front of the green. For Nicklaus, this was the golf tournament.

Well, he nailed it. For all of those 240 yards, the shot was right on the flag. The ball landed softly and came to rest pin-high, only 15 feet from the cup. It wasn't a double eagle, of course. It wasn't even an eagle, for the putt slid just around the lip, but it was an easy two-putt birdie—and the blow that actually won him that Masters.

For the history books, Jack gave that 1-iron shot the description it deserved. "Best pressure shot of my life," he would say.

There is yet another Nicklaus moment that is *italicized* and **boldfaced** in my memory, though it's a moment of a slightly different nature. I take you to Muirfield in Scotland, British Open, final round, 1972.

The Grand Slam had slowly slipped away from Nicklaus through three rounds when he had played too cautiously, too conservatively, but suddenly he was retrieving it. He had taken out the driver and attacked the course. He was a blazing six under through ten holes. He had caught the leaders, Lee Trevino and Tony Jacklin. He now had the crowd with him. Overcome by the roars of encouragement from the stampeding throngs, he confessed later that he was behooved to wipe away a tear of emotion as he walked down the eleventh fairway.

But that's not the moment. The moment came at the fifteenth green, where Jack rapped a simple, straight-in, 8-foot birdie putt into the heart of the cup to go seven under—and uncatchable, no doubt—but the putt didn't drop. The ball didn't spin or lip out. Nothing like that. And it wasn't stroked too hard, it was stroked perfectly, but the putt flat refused to go in. The ball virtually seemed to float across the center of the cup, and it wound up sitting on the back edge. It was as if destiny had decided that it would have more to say about things than Jack Nicklaus, for a change.

A short time later that afternoon, destiny did in fact choose Lee Trevino as the winner of that intensely exciting and totally bizarre British Open.

Several years later in one of those sit-around, remember-when sessions with Jack, I brought up that short birdie putt on the fifteenth green at Muirfield, saying it looked from where I was standing that day that he had put it right in the throat—I couldn't believe the ball had stayed out.

With something of a sigh, Jack said, "It didn't hit anything but air."

In his prime, during all his best years, Nicklaus never missed many putts that he needed to make. It's an absolute truth that nobody ever made as many putts that he *had* to make, in dire situations, in critical moments, in large events, as Jack Nicklaus. I mean, the guy sank crucial, killer putts for twenty years!

I brought this up on another occasion one evening when we were having a chat. I was hoping to draw from him some deep, dark secret about his putting. How could he explain it? Sheer luck? God's chosen golfer? What?

He mulled it over for a moment, and finally looked at me in his matter-of-fact way, and said, "I've never missed a putt in my *mind*."

Yeah. The minute he said it, I thought the same thing.

Golf lesson, comma.

PART ONE

The Way It Is Today— Dining Out on Corporate Logos

The Best Things in Golf

TELL ME ABOUT PLUMBING, fine. How if this fitting doesn't go into that pipe, my bathroom looks like the Danube. Tell me about carpentry, terrace gardening, the timer on VCRs. Go ahead and explain cellophane—and why I can't open a package of crackers without a chain saw. Tell me about all of these things, but don't try to tell me about golf, okay? Golf I know.

For one thing, I'm older than beltless slacks and twice as old as tassel loafers. For another thing, I've been covering golf since the glory days, when a touring pro only had a set of clubs and a caddy instead of a lawyer, an agent, a business manager, and a guru.

You don't have to back me into a corner to get me to tell you I've seen more major championships over these past forty years than Irving Berlin saw piano keys.

Listened to golf? I've heard more golf stories than a Bolshoi dancer has heard *Swan Lake*.

Played golf? I've played every great course from Goat Hills to Augusta National, from Pine Valley to St. Andrews, from Pebble Beach to Seminole. I've played rounds of golf with Ben Hogan, Arnold Palmer, and Jack Nicklaus, just to drop three names at random, and I used to play at scratch from the blues and gamble for my own money when I didn't have any, so don't tell me about pressure either.

All of which makes me the only person I know who is qualified to pick the Best Things in Golf, which I will now present:

BEST FIRST TEE

Merion. This elegant and shady patch of ground out there on Philadelphia's Main Line is impossible to gaze upon without thinking that, yeah, here's where Bobby Jones teed it up on the morning of the Amateur final in 1930 when he was about to complete that Grand Slam thing.

BEST VERANDA

The Augusta National, which also has the Best Driveway (Magnolia), the Best Creek (Rae's), and the Best Balcony (main clubhouse), which overlooks the Best Veranda.

BEST PUTTING GREEN

Has to be Oakmont. Hard by the huge old clubhouse in a suburb of Pittsburgh, this putting green actually connects with the par-5 ninth green. Very unique. All in all, it looks like the world's largest bent-grass farm.

BEST BRIDGE

No contest. The Swinging Bridge at the Bel Air Country Club. It takes you over a canyon to the tenth green, a par 3, and has held the cleats of the most movie stars.

BEST BAR

Downstairs in the Pebble Beach Lodge, a small, dark, cozy, convivial room called Club XIX. Famous faces come and go, if you're into that. First barstool on the right deserves to have my name on it, in brass. Some say this watering hole is expensive, but if you didn't know that, what are you doing at Pebble Beach in the first place?

BEST TROPHY ROOM

Ben Hogan's alcove. It's just off the big main room as you enter the Colonial Country Club in Fort Worth. Three walls of display cases filled with everything from his early junior golf days to all the big stuff. Trophies, medals, and plaques galore. My favorite jewelry store.

BEST SHORT PAR 3

The twelfth at Augusta National. Only a short iron over water but the scene of countless tragicomedies during the Masters.

BEST LONG PAR 3

The sixteenth at Cypress Point. You can top your drive but you can't top the scenery.

BEST SHORT PAR 4

The eighth at Pine Valley. Put it down the hill on this dogleg right and you're left with only a wedge to a green guarded by bunkers, except that the green is only the size of a dinner plate. Actually, that's an exaggeration—it's more the size of an ashtray.

BEST LONG PAR 4

There's no such thing if you're trying to play golf. But

press me on the subject and I'll give you the seventeenth at St. Andrews, the Road Hole.

BEST PAR 5

The thirteenth at Augusta National. Sharp dogleg left, Rae's Creek beckons all the way to the green, a bank of azaleas for set decoration, and you can go for it in two or not.

BEST TWO HOLES IN A ROW

The twelfth and thirteenth at Augusta.

BEST THREE HOLES IN A ROW

The eleventh, twelfth, and thirteenth at Augusta, Amen Corner.

BEST THREE HOLES IN A ROW THAT AREN'T AT AUGUSTA

The eighth, ninth, and tenth at Pebble Beach, Abalone Corner. My name, copyrighted.

BEST FIVE HOLES IN A ROW

The thirteenth through the seventeenth at Black Diamond Ranch down near Ocala, Florida. You play around a deep quarry, which has now unseated Merion for Best Quarry.

BEST EIGHTEEN HOLES IN A ROW

Pine Valley. Amid gorgeous, haunting scenery in Clementon, New Jersey, each hole is exquisite and memorable, if, at times, utterly impossible.

BEST RULE IN GOLF

That thing about the burrowing animal, whatever it means.

BEST SHOTMAKER

Ben Hogan, you needed to ask?

BEST SWING

Sam Snead.

BEST DRIVER

Hogan.

BEST LONG-IRON PLAYER

Jack Nicklaus. He was the first to get them up, keep them up, turn them either way, keep them on the greens.

BEST SHORT IRONS

Byron Nelson.

BEST CHIPPER

Raymond Floyd.

BEST WIND PLAYER

Lee Trevino, who learned to play in the Texas gales, for his own money.

BEST PUTTER

Ben Crenshaw, who invented the 15-foot gimme.

BEST PLAYER WHO NEVER HIT A FAIRWAY OFF THE TEE

Seve Ballesteros.

BEST GOLFER IN A COAT AND TIE

Harry Vardon, evidently.

BEST PLAYER WHO NEVER WORE PANTS

Gene Sarazen.

BEST GRINDER

Tom Kite. He can outwork a dozen heavy-lifters and has the bank account to show for it.

BEST GOLFER WHO NEVER PRACTICED

Jimmy Demaret. It cut into party time.

BEST LADY GOLFER
Babe Zaharias, in a playoff over Mickey Wright.

BEST PLAYER WHO STOPPED TO SMELL THE FLOWERS
Walter Hagen.

BEST GOLFER I NEVER SAW PLAY
Bobby Jones.

BEST GOLFER WHO USED TO SMOKE, SWEAT, LET HIS SHIRTTAIL COME OUT
Arnold Palmer.

BEST TOURING PRO WHO EVER PICKED UP DINNER CHECKS
Dave Marr.

BEST COLOR-BLIND GOLFER WHO USED AN INTERLOCKING GRIP
Jack Nicklaus.

BEST GOLFER WHO NEVER DIED
Sam Snead. Nobody else ever won tournaments in *six* different decades.

BEST THING ANY GOLFER EVER SAID ABOUT THE PRESS
"Whatever amount of fame I have achieved from the relatively unimportant pursuit of hitting a golf ball, I owe to O. B. Keeler and his gifted typewriter." — Bobby Jones.

BEST LEAD EVER WRITTEN ON A GOLF STORY
Not many arguments about this. Most of us who have been around a while tend to give the honor to the late Leonard Crawley of London's *Daily Telegraph,* who once wrote:

"Despite the abominable handling of the press luggage at the Zurich airport, the Swiss Open managed to get off to a rather decent start yesterday."

The Host Club

AS A FAIRLY ENTHUSIASTIC recreational golfer, I was naturally excited when a PGA Tour event came to my country cub. I dashed right out there, not only to pick up some swing tips from the pros but to see all of the famous stars in their own flesh and blood and square grooves.

The first shock came when I was forced to park on a school playground five miles away, ride a shuttle bus, and then buy a badge just to get into my own country club. The badge cost $5,000 but the money was for charity, somebody said.

The club sure looked different. A lot of big trucks and mobile homes were sitting around, circus tents had been put up, and a good many wives of members I knew were wearing the same bonnets, blouses, and polka-dot skirts, and were hastily jumping in and out of white Buicks.

"Hi, Mildred," I said. "Where's Fred?"

"I can't talk now," she said, panting. "Mark Brooks needs to go to the dentist and Scott Simpson has to find a discount store." She sped away in the courtesy car.

My next shock came when I entered the clubhouse and a security guard refused to admit me to my own locker room.

"I wish you wouldn't push me in the chest," I said, trying to smile.

"Players and officials only," he said gruffly.

"I'm a member," I said.

"Move along, please. Can't you see how crowded this hallway is?"

"I want to use the bathroom," I explained.

The security guard spoke into a walkie-talkie.

"Ralph, we've got a code three in the locker area. Want to send some help down here to get the asshole out? Over."

I got the point and went downstairs to the Men's Grill to grab a bite to eat. There was another security guard on the door.

"Wrong badge," he said, stopping me.

"This is supposed to be good for the clubhouse," I said, fondling the badge pinned to my shirt.

"You're not a Patron."

"A what?"

"Patrons only. Sorry."

"How do you get to be a Patron?" I asked.

"You buy a Patron's badge for ten thousand dollars."

I thought I might find a snack in the Mixed Four-some Room, but, alas, I ran into another security guard.

He shoved me backward.

"My wife and I play bridge in this room," I said.

"You're not a Saint."

"A what?"

"This room is for Saints only."

"What does it cost to be a Saint?"

"I think it's twenty thousand dollars, but you get a seat on the eighteenth fairway along with it."

The next place I looked for food was the teenage rec-reation parlor, which our club calls the Peppermint Lounge.

Yet another security guard was on the door.

I peeked around him and noticed several men and women with cocktails in their hands, while others were loading up their plates at a sumptuous buffet.

"Press only," the security guard said.

"The tournament's outside," I argued.

"They bring the leaders in here to be interviewed," he informed me. "Clear the doorway, please. Larry Nelson is on his way here."

It turned out that the only place where a clubhouse badge holder could find food was in the lobby, along with 4,000 other people. I stood in line for two hours and finally got a fat roast-beef sandwich and a warm Coke.

"I'll just sign for this," I said when I reached the cashier.

"You need scrip," the lady said.

"I need what?"

"Members can't sign this week. You have to buy scrip. I have a twenty-dollar book for a hundred dollars or a forty-dollar book for five hundred dollars."

Giving up on food, I went outside to watch the tour-nament. At the ninth green, I squeezed into a throng of 10,000 people and caught a glimpse of three golfers down on their hands and knees, evidently staring at in-sects.

"Which one's Nicklaus?" I asked a fellow spectator.

"Nicklaus doesn't play in this tournament," he said.

Moments later, another group of golfers came to the ninth hole. Mostly, they walked around in circles and held their putters out in front of them, vertically, and squinted.

"Is this Watson?" I inquired.

"Watson never plays here," I was told.

"He doesn't?"

"Naw. Neither does Trevino, or Crenshaw, or Norman, or Zoeller. Palmer plays here, though."

"Great," I said. "When's Arnie coming up?"

"He's not here this year."

I asked which of the famous players *were* here.

The man said, "Well, that's David Ogrin in the bunker. Bob Lohr's the guy behind the tree trunk. Wayne Grady's waiting on a ruling about the water."

The player I most wanted to watch was Nick Faldo, the greatest golfer in the world. A woman told me she thought Faldo was on the back nine.

I walked out to the fourteenth hole, the farthest point from the clubhouse. There were maybe a dozen fans watching three players who were identified to me as Tim Simpson, Ronnie Black, and Joe Don Blake.

"I guess Faldo will be coming up pretty soon, huh?" I said to a man sitting under a tree.

"Not this year," the man said. "Faldo can't play in the United States, except in four or five tournaments. Our pros voted on it."

"That's ridiculous," I said, exhausted, hungry, thirsty. "Why am I at this golf tournament if there are no players I've ever heard of?"

"Beats me," the man said. "I'm just sitting here till the goddamn thing's over. The committee closed the street in front of my house and I don't have the right badge to get back home."

Designers
and Developers

EXCUSE ME, I didn't mean to yawn, but I was just sitting here trying to remember the last time I ran into an old friend who wasn't designing a new golf course somewhere and participating in the real estate development around it.

My old friend Jim is a good example. I bumped into Jim in an airport lobby the other day.

"How's it going, Jim?" I said.

"Great! I'm designing a new golf course and I've got a piece of the real estate deal."

"What happened to the brokerage business?"

"You ought to see the land we've got," Jim said. "Our money people say it's the best parcel they ever acquired."

"Where is it?"

"Tristan da Cunha."

"Mexico?"

"No, it's south of the equator. An island."

"I get it," I said. "Go to Rio de Janeiro and take a left."

"You could. It's probably easier if you go to Cape Town and take a right. You won't believe what our money people have planned for this place. Hotels, condos, villas, three-acre lots. The landing strip will be ready next year."

"Sounds like paradise," I said. "How do you get there now? Shipwreck?"

"Hovercraft. There are two a week from Queen Maud."

"Queen Maud in Antarctica?"

"Yeah, on a clear day, you can see Antarctica."

"I guess we're talking about a second-home development, huh?"

"Third home," he said. "Our money people say it's all over for the second-home market. You can't get a tee time anywhere."

I asked Jim what he was going to name the course.

"St. Andrews at Tristan da Cunha," he said, rushing off to hug an Arab.

I went to a pay phone, which is where I bumped into my old friend Tom. I asked Tom what was up.

"Everything!" He was beaming. "I'm designing a new golf course and I've got a piece of the real estate deal."

"What happened to the fast-food business?"

"You ought to see the land we've got," Tom said. "Our money people say it's the most fantastic acreage they've ever leased. Half of it's in Wyoming, the other half's in Montana. Our money people are talking about three luxury hotels, five hundred town houses, two hundred club villas, and a marina. No homesites. It's all over for primary residences. People want no worries, they want recreation. A marina's the key."

"If a marina's the key, what are you doing in Wyoming and Montana?"

"Hey, pal, do I look stupid?" said Tom. "Wait till you see the lake we're gonna build!"

"What are you calling the place?"

"St. Andrews at Little Bighorn," he said, dashing away to hug two Japanese gentlemen.

The car-rental counter is where I bumped into my old friend Ken.

"Hi, Ken, how you doing?"

"Couldn't be better," he said. "I'm designing a new golf course and I've got a piece of the real estate deal."

"What happened to the roofing business?"

"You ought to see this piece of property we've got. Our money people say it has more potential than anything they've ever looked at. You know Toledo, Ohio, right?"

"Not intimately."

"You know where the interstate curves around after it passes the jeep plant? Stay to the right. Don't go downtown. Exit at the Sheraton. Go to the shopping strip on your right. Behind the Kmart? That's the first fairway. Par five."

"It is?"

"Second hole is a blind par three. You hit over the discount drugstore. I'm pretty excited."

"I can see why. Where are the condos and villas?"

"All underground."

"I'm sorry," I said. "I thought for a minute you said they were underground."

"Every unit," he said. "Our money people say it's all over for inconvenience. You walk out of your living room, go up an escalator, you're on the first tee. Come off of eighteen, you buy wicker furniture, eat Chinese, go to Adult Video, take the escalator home. People want to golf where they shop."

"Does the club have a name?"

"St. Andrews at Spark Plug Mall! We broke concrete this week."

I wished Ken luck and told him in all sincerity that I'd like to meet his money people someday.

"You'll love 'em," he said. "Two guys from Dallas. They used to be in the savings and loan business."

"He's Safely On"

THERE HAS always been a good deal of evidence that when it comes to announcing golf on television, it pays to be uninformed. Note that I am too nice a fellow to have said stupid.

One of the more obvious examples came in a recent spring when a network announcer, whose name I will withhold out of sympathy for his family, referred to the venue of the Ryder Cup Matches—the Belfry—as being located in the town of "Coldfield Sutton, England."

This was the equivalent of saying "Diego San, California," or "Worth Fort, Texas."

I would have been willing to ignore this as a slip of the tongue, perhaps caused by a demented director screaming something inane in the announcer's earpiece, if it hadn't been said three times over two different telecasts, and was never corrected on the air.

The mistake would not have seemed so grievous if Sutton Coldfield had not become rather famous. It was, after all, the place where the Europeans startled the world by defeating the U.S.A. in the 1985 Ryder Cup, and then startled the world again by retaining the 1989 Ryder Cup in one of the most thrilling competitions— a dramatic tie—of the past several golfing decades.

Golf writers make errors, too, but they are usually of a less glaring nature. We may say that someone hit a 1-iron when in reality it was a 4-wood, but at least we know the player used a golf club and not a polo mallet.

We may reflect on John Daly winning the PGA in Indianapolis in 1992 when it was actually in 1991, but at least we will have the player, the city, and the championship correct—and whiskey, not ignorance, to blame for the lost year.

I know of no writer who ever wrote, even under the influence, that Floyd Raymond won the Open National at the Hills of Shinnecock on Island Long, York New.

But of course we put up with various intellectual comments from these announcers on a weekly basis. I give you:

• **He has a lot of green to work with.** Yes, he does. I wonder what all he's going to do before he hits the pitch. Oh, I expect he will aerate the green first, then verti-cut it. He knows all about this, being in the golf course design business when he's not playing the PGA Tour. Oops, the ball seems to have pulled up 20 feet short of the cup. Guess he forgot he had overseeded it while he was thinking about all the green he had to work with.

• **He'll have this tap-in for his par.** Ever since network announcers invented the three-foot tap-in many years ago, golfers have been looking for it. They have found the three-foot three-putt, even the two-foot three-putt, but they have yet to come across the three-foot tap-in. They know it's out there somewhere—the networks have told them it is, so it must be true.

• **I'll be reporting from the 398-yard par-4 sixteenth hole, a dogleg left with an undulating green.** Right. Where, to date, you've seen 38 pars, 276 birdies, 497 bogeys, and 59 double bogeys posted by golfers ranging in height from five-five to six-two with an average weight of 186 pounds. In addition, most of them have missed putts from 27½ feet, although some have made putts from 16½ feet.

• **It was a diabolical shot but, oh dear, he's been consigned to a watery grave.** The token Brit. "Jolly good fun to be here, I must say. And what marvelous stuff we're seeing from these lads as they nestle their wedges up to the old flags. Oh, well now, a bit too much muscle on that one, I daresay, but all in all, rather a good shot from a sticky lie."

• **That was a good play from there.** In my experience, a good play was generally written by Noël Coward or Tennessee Williams, but I have seen other good ones by Tom Stoppard and David Mamet.

I have yet to see a good play in a golf tournament, but I'm hopeful that one of these days I will be watching when Nick Price tucks the ball under his arm, stiff-arms Bernhard Langer, sidesteps Seve Ballesteros, and dashes 347 yards for a birdie.

• **He shouldn't have much trouble getting up and down from there.** Oh? I can almost swear the ball is sitting in sand, 10 feet below a bulkhead, 30 yards from the flag.

But I guess the announcer is right. As we know, these fellows are all brain surgeons. Oops, he seems to have left it in the bunker. Probably wasn't his best effort, although he's a fine young man.

• **He's a fine young man.** Except when he's around a golf writer. The last time any of us saw him, he was sullen, uncooperative, complaining about the golf course, and refusing to sign an autograph for a paraplegic.

• **He's safely on.** Right. After hitting the worst choke-gouge 9-iron in history, he has a triple-breaking, uphill-downhill 60-footer, but he's safely on.

• **And let's don't forget that Greg Norman is still in the hunt.** I won't. And if Greg can throw a little 27 at 'em on the back nine, he can move into a tie for twelfth.

• **It's absolutely amazing how much talent these fellows have.** It certainly is. With the hot ball, the graphite shaft, the metal woods, the perfectly maintained fairways, and the true-putting greens, I'm constantly amazed at how they can play golf almost as well as Hogan Ben, Snead Sam, and Nelson Byron.

Bobby Joe Grooves

I CAUGHT UP with Bobby Joe Grooves in Logo, California, not long ago as he stood in front of the clubhouse and complained about the color of his courtesy car.

It was a white Buick, not the blue one he had asked for.

"And look at this," he said, opening the trunk. "It's too small. How am I supposed to get $537,000 in here? These sponsors better get on the ball if they expect me to come back to *this* cesspool next year."

Bobby Joe had just won the $537,000 by finishing in a tie for nineteenth place in the Chrysler/Shearson/Nissan/Kmart/McDonald's/Taco Bell Classic at L'Arbitrage Country Club. He had asked for the prize money in small unmarked bills, a habit he acquired in a prior profession.

Despite the fact that the car was the wrong color, Bobby Joe planned to drive it to the next stop on the PGA Tour, which was the Isuzu/Kemper/Wendy's/Sony/Insurance Agent Classic in San Logo, Florida.

That's where he would leave the courtesy car in a ditch, and become the first player on the tour to leave twelve consecutive courtesy cars in ditches.

Bobby Joe said there was no question that some of the new rules on the tour were helping him make a living, although he had not come close to winning a tournament. He especially liked the new changes in the distribution of prize money. The difference between first place and tenth place was now only $7.16.

"That's the way it should be," Bobby Joe said. "If it wasn't for me and a lot of other guys like me out here, Jack Nicklaus wouldn't have anybody to beat."

Bobby Joe is only five-four and weighs only 150 pounds but he is one of the longest hitters on the tour, and I assumed it had something to do with the new technology.

I said, "Let's talk about the clubs you use, the ball you play."

"That's kind of personal."

"It's pretty common knowledge that your grooves are going to be declared illegal someday," I said.

"That's really a crock, too." He frowned. "I'm talking to my lawyer about it."

"Is it true that Greg Norman's teeth put the grooves in your irons."

"Yeah, so what? Greg's a friend of mine."

"Where did you get the idea for the plutonium shaft in your driver?"

"Simple. I saw this show on TV about the H-bomb."

I told him I'd learned from the manufacturer that the club head was made of granite molded around the core of a month-old grilled cheese sandwich.

"You're not going to print that, are you?" he asked warily.

"Let's talk about the grip," I said. "I understand you've signed a contract to endorse the condom grip."

"It's a pretty good deal," he said.

"The grip is a combination of unborn lamb and Krazy Glue, right?"

"I guess. All I know is, your hands don't slip."

"You're definitely getting great distance off the tee. Is it primarily the ball you're using?"

"Depends on where you get your specimen."

"What do you mean?"

"Hey, man, we all carry a hypodermic needle out here. One day I took a sample out of Watson's ball, put it in my own. Talk about hot."

"Are you saying Tom Watson plays a hot ball?"

"Does the Pope wear a cross?"

I had one last question. I had seen Bobby Joe quoted as saying God had helped him become a better player.

"God?" he said. "You mean like . . . up there?"

"Yes."

"Uh . . . right," he said. "God helped me get through the Q school, but I don't know that He helps me so much anymore. Like on the first hole today, after my drive. I'd like to have seen God try to hit a 3-iron out of that divot *I* was in."

I thanked him for his time. He said I shouldn't forget to write that he was just out here trying to make a living for his family.

What If the Tour Stopped Tomorrow?

IT SEEMS like a good idea occasionally to remind Bobby Joe Grooves and some of his pals on the PGA Tour that there's no law that says there has to be a PGA Tour. The tour always was, and still is, a total accident— like oysters, or two-putting from 40 feet.

I don't mean to send Bobby Joe into shock but the tour could disappear tomorrow and it would not be the end of the world, or even golf. The tour is not golf. About twenty million recreational golfers happen to be golf, and besides that, there would still be a Masters, a U.S. Open, a British Open, and a PGA, which are the only newsworthy tournaments anyhow.

The only time normal, everyday, run-of-the-mill tour events are important is when Byron Nelson wins eleven of them in a row.

The majors have nothing to do with the tour, seeing as how they are presided over by other organizations, and seeing as how three of them, the U.S. Open, the British Open, and the PGA were around before there even *was* a tour, or even the steel shaft.

If there was no tour today, would golf heroes still emerge? Certainly.

Francis Ouimet put golf on the front page around the world by beating Harry Vardon and Ted Ray in a playoff for the U.S. Open in 1913, not by winning the Massachusetts Invitational.

Bobby Jones didn't become an immortal by winning the Catalina Open, or even playing in it.

Walter Hagen didn't become a household name by winning the Gasparilla Open.

Gene Sarazen didn't become a star by winning the West Coast of Florida Open.

It's the majors that make golf reputations. Ask Ben Hogan. Ask Arnold Palmer. Ask Jack Nicklaus. Better still, ask Sam Snead. Sam won eleven tournaments in 1950 but most of them happened to be the Reading Open, so Hogan was voted Player of the Year for winning the U.S. Open.

You may ask what the tour was to speak of before there was a tour to speak of. It was largely a handful of winter events called the First Stoplight in Coral Gables Open at which Walter Hagen and a few friends competed to see who bought supper in the diner. They passed a hat to raise prize money and after a few weeks they went to their regular jobs as club pros.

The tour remained primarily a winter thing until the 1930s when first a man named Bob Harlow and then a man named Fred Corcoran became the tournament manager for the PGA of America. This is what the commissioner's job was called before Deane Beman enlarged the job so much that it required a CEO, like him.

Corcoran built the modern tour as we know it. He did it by scaring up rich and influential gentlemen in various cities who loved golf. "Put up some money for a tournament," Fred would say. "I'll bring Hogan, Snead, Nelson, and Demaret. Hogan will invent practice, Snead will invent the picture swing, Nelson will win, and Demaret will tell jokes."

"What's in it for me?" the man would ask.

Fred would think a minute, and say, "I'll get your picture taken with Snead."

It was a deal.

Hence, the sponsor was born. And the sponsor hasn't changed much over the years. He still gets his picture taken with the stars and enjoys sniffing around their pant legs.

Personally, I find the recent history of the San Diego Open, just to cite one example, to be as intriguing as anything Fred Corcoran did.

In 1981 it was called the Wickes/Andy Williams Open. In 1983 it became the Isuzu/Andy Williams Open. In 1986 it was the Shearson Lehman Brothers/Andy Williams Open. In 1988 it was the Shearson Lehman/Hutton/Andy Williams Open. In 1989 it was the Shearson Lehman/Hutton Open. In 1991 it was the Shearson Lehman Brothers Open. In 1992 it was the Buick Invitational of California.

Correct me if I'm wrong, but I believe that over the same period of time, the U.S. Open, the British Open, the Masters, and the PGA continued to be known as the U.S. Open, the British Open, the Masters, and the PGA.

In case Bobby Joe Grooves and his pals haven't figured out by now how the tour could disappear someday, I will tell them.

It could happen if all of the sponsors suddenly decided they were sick and tired of raising millions of dollars in prize money to give away to a group of guys for the only three things they normally get in return, which are (a) having to track down courtesy cars that Bobby Joe and his friends have left in ditches, (b) watching Bobby Joe and his friends refuse to speak to their pro-am partners, and (c) hearing from Bobby Joe and his friends that downtown Beirut is in better condition than this lousy golf course they're trying to play.

It's something for Bobby Joe and the others to think about while they are—somewhere, right now—complaining about the salad on the free lunch in the clubhouse.

Tour Pro Seeks
New Line of Work

I'LL TELL YOU one thing. I've three-jacked it for the last time and missed the cut and had my heart broke on this PGA Tour. You can just write it up in your paper right now that Bobby Joe Grooves is sick and tired of seeing nothin' on the tour but a bunch of no-name psychos who go at the flag on every shot and one-jack it on every green, even when they have to putt it over divots, spike marks, and insects.

So I'm goin' into the private sector, is where I'm goin'. I'm gonna get me one of them platinum parachute deals like all the sponsors have, then I won't have to steer-job a tee ball or cold-jump a 2-iron no more. It shouldn't be too hard for a touring pro with a marquee name like mine to find an executive position.

I asked around, and this PPL (Platinum Parachute Lightweight) told me I needed a résumé. I said I didn't speak French—what's a résumé? He told me what it was and what it ought to look like. You read mine and if you have any ideas about what might make it look more impressive, drop me a line.

Bobby Joe Grooves

Present Address

c/o Miss Dorene Branch, 3916 Airport Drive, No. B-6, Atlanta, Ga.

Permanent Address

c/o Miss Patti Trickster, 919 Alligator Circle, Palm Clump, Fla.

Objective

To obtain a vice president's job, or some kind of fake deal like that.

Education

Aug. 30–Sept. 26, 1985. Southeast Florida University. Major: Golf Team. Minor: Stereo Repair.

Oct. 15–Nov. 10, 1985. Georgia Cumberland College. Major: Chip Shots. Minor: Side Bets.

Jan. 10–Feb. 22, 1986. Alabama Christian Institute. Major: Discovered the school didn't have a golf team, left.

Sept. 15–Oct. 5, 1986. Southern North Carolina Tech. Major: Bent Greens. Minor: Bermuda Greens.

March 10–April 1, 1986. University of Houston. Major: Would have been Marketing if I had not been falsely arrested for auto theft and kicked off golf team. Minor: Would have been Psychology or Religion.

Experience

Jan. 7–May 10, 1987. Popeye's, Jacksonville, Fla. Inventory control of red beans and rice.

June 6–June 23, 1987. Lake Ruth Recreational Center, Big Mouth, Tex. Lifeguard and waterfront director.

July 9–Aug. 17, 1987. Grady's Paint & Body, Amarillo, Tex. Customer service and manual labor.

Oct. 3–Dec. 13, 1987. Mack's Bibles 'n' Things, Montgomery, Ala. Cold-call selling.

Jan. 15–Nov. 10, 1988. Roy's Discount Golf, Okeechewchow, Fla. Assembly and retail sales.

Nov. 15–Nov. 22, 1988. PGA Qualifying School, TPC at Osprey Dump, S.C. Shot lights out, finished third, should have led, and found innocent of cheating charges.

Feb. 21–Feb. 24, 1989. Hiroshima Los Angeles Open, Pacific Palisades, Calif. Finished twelfth but should have won.

March 7–March 15, 1989. Took time off to marry Betty Lou Dibbs, the girl of my dreams.

March 21–March 24, 1989. Nagasaki New Orleans Classic, Doo, La. Finished second because winner got free drop on last hole.

April 11–April 14, 1989. Tojo Hirohito Heritage, Hilton Head, S.C. Three-putted last six holes for twenty-second place.

May 16–May 19, 1989. Takaichi Hyuga Memorial, Dublin, Ohio. Hit sprinkler head on perfect 5-iron shot, missed cut.

June 16–June 19, 1989. U.S. Open, Silly Oak Country Club, Grand Rural, N.Y. Missed cut because of stupid high rough. Last time the USGA will see my butt again.

July 1–Dec. 30, 1989. Took rest of year off to assess future and divorce that low-rent scag, Betty Lou Dibbs.

Jan. 10–Jan. 13, 1990. Tatsunoke Niching Tucson Open, TPC at Reptile Desert, Ariz. Three-putted twelve times. Switched to Ping.

Feb. 1–May 1, 1990. Took time off to work with David Leadbetter.

May 7–May 10, 1990. Mutsuki Hiroyishi Atlanta Classic,

TPC at Barbecue Fork, Ga. Developed severe slice, finished ninth.

May 15–July 1, 1990. Took time off to work with Harvey Penick.

July 13–July 16, 1990. Mitsuru Ozawa Hartford Open, TPC at Fine Print, Conn. Developed severe shank. WD, quit game indefinitely.

Activities

Fellowship of Christian Athletes; founding member of Pi Sig Ep Golf Fraternity at Georgia Cumberland College.

References

Warden J. J. Hobby—Oakdale Federal Correctional Facility. Others available on request.

Media Messages

IT WAS a matter of pure coincidence that just as I was preparing to write a magazine article about the new Foot-Joy Sta-Sof glove that stays soft twice as long and improves your grip by 50 percent, I happened to open this letter from an angry reader somewhere in Ohio and discovered that the gentleman likes corporate logos.

He first accused me of being a "crybaby" about all of the logos on the PGA Tour. He then called me a "hypocrite" because magazines and newspapers sell advertising in their pages, which, if I understood him correctly, keeps me from having to wear a sign around my neck that says: "I Write for Food."

He reminded me that corporate logos pay all the bills on the PGA Tour. The logos didn't bother *him,* he said, so why should they bother *me*? Without the corporate logos, he was certain, there would be no golf tournaments on TV for him to watch.

I should stop messing around with his fun, he said, because there was no difference between me writing for a magazine that sold ads and a touring pro picking up a check from a corporate sponsor.

Well, how to respond?

To begin with, I suppose, I should say that all of the above sentences were brought to you by the Buick Le-Sabre, which offers the safety of antilock brakes as well as an interior that now gives you even greater front headroom and rear legroom.

I have more to say on the subject, but first I feel the need to mention that this paragraph is sponsored by Pioneer, the Art of Entertainment, which has the most accurate color and the sharpest picture of any big-screen TV.

Not that I watch much golf on TV anymore, unless I think there might be more fascinating commercial interruptions than usual.

But let me get back to the point, which ties in with Etonic's Dri-Tech XT Plus golf shoes that are built with Etonic's exclusive XT-Loc Spike System and ceramic-tipped spikes.

I am well aware that I have complained excessively about this logo thing, but I never thought it made me sound like a crybaby. I merely thought it made me sound like an acute sufferer of nostalgia, to remember with particular fondness those classier, happier days when golf tournaments were named for cities, country clubs, and people instead of the manufacturers of fully digital communications systems.

Incidentally, I've changed my mind about something as I sit here typing. I used to urge newspaper and magazine editors to do the PGA Tour a favor and continue referring to events in print by their old names—the Tucson Open, the Colonial National Invitation, the New Orleans Open, what have you. It would help preserve their dignity. Suddenly, now, it's come to me that in this free society, a tournament has the right to call itself whatever it wishes, no matter how silly or idiotic it sounds.

You may ask what all that has to do with Ernest & Julio Gallo's Sauvignon Blanc having a crisp, clean taste and being a natural complement to today's cuisine, or with Mitsubishi introducing its Montero with Active Trac four-wheel drive, a new shift-on-the-fly system that can be optimized for any driving condition, while you were thinking about the U.S. Open result.

I have the answer. It opens up a whole new world of golf writing . . .

BY A REPRESENTATIVE OF THE TRAVELERS
Where you're better off under the umbrella

PEBBLE BEACH, Calif. (AP) — While the Cadillac De-ville minimized wheel slip as you accelerated for greater control, and while Motorola was on your mind when you wanted the convenience of a cellular phone, a Titleist HVC with a cutproof Lithium Surlyn cover won the U.S. Open today when a golfer putted it into the cup on the last hole.

I can't say I would look forward to working in that journalistic climate, but I'm sure it wouldn't bother the logo lovers in the least.

The Man Himself

THIS WILL introduce you to a golf celebrity of sorts, Billy Ray Johnny Jack Joe Bob Bubbajim, 47, part-time roofer, the first daily-ticket buyer on the PGA Tour to holler, "You the man."

Billy Ray Johnny Jack Joe Bob decided it was time to make his name known to the public. That's why he called to ask if I wanted an exclusive interview.

"You the man?" I asked. "Really?"

"You talkin' to him right now today," he said.

Billy Ray Johnny Jack Joe Bob explained that he wanted to reveal his identity to the world because two of his friends around his hometown of Bunker Rake, Georgia, were claiming credit for it.

"They wasn't first to yell it by no means," he said, "and they fixin' to dig a pitchin' wedge out of their ear if they keep on braggin' about it."

He suggested we have lunch to talk in depth. I agreed when I learned the restaurant of his choice wasn't too far from my home in north Florida.

He said he would be wearing his favorite golf cap, the blue one that said, I'M A GIMME—PICK ME UP, DARLIN', and his favorite T-shirt, the orange one that read, WHAT ARE YOU LOOKIN' AT, SHANKFACE?

The restaurant was located on I-95, halfway between Brunswick and Savannah. Billy Ray Johnny Jack Joe Bob had promised that it catered to golf lovers. It was called Big Bertha's.

I found Billy Ray Johnny Jack Joe Bob sitting in a booth, joined him and ordered a Coke. "Small, medium, or large?" asked the waitress, Brenda Fay Norma Jane Reba Diane.

I looked around at some other customers and realized that the small Coke came in a carton the size of a bucket for practice balls, the medium Coke came in a carton the size of a tour pro's golf bag, and the large Coke came in a carton the size of a putter barrel.

"I'll just have coffee," I said.

"Decaf or blue tees?"

"Whichever one I can lift," I said.

Billy Ray Johnny Jack Joe Bob recommended three delicacies on Big Bertha's menu. The Hook & Slice was a barbecue platter with two whole chickens and a slab of ribs served with ice tongs and a machete. The Fairways & Greens was a lettuce-and-tomato salad, richly flavored with Florida lottery tickets. The Nestled Wedge was a sausage biscuit inside a quadruple-decker cheeseburger.

We got down to business and I asked Billy Ray Johnny Jack Joe Bob if he had been a golf fan all his life.

"I've spent every dollar I ever made on golf," he said. "I've got six ex-wives you can check out on that deal."

Could he remember the first tournament where he yelled, "You the man"?

"Absolutely," he said. "It was four years ago over there at Harbert Town. I yelled it out when I seen that old boy, Ed Couples, hit a 300-yard 7-iron."

"Don't you mean Fred Couples?"

"Ever what his name is. He was paired with old David Love."

I asked, "Have you always hollered things at golf tournaments?"

"You bet," he said. "I don't see no point in goin' to a golf tournament if you can't holler nothin'."

"What did you use to holler before you started hollering, 'You the man'?"

"I can tell you exactly. All through them 1960s and 1970s, I hollered, 'Go, Arnie.'"

"I seem to recall a lot of people were hollering, 'Go Arnie' at the time."

"Yeah, but I hollered it louder. See, when I'm at a golf tournament, I can holler louder than one of them used-car salesmen on TV. Of course, I had to stop hollerin' it when Arnie stopped going nowhere in particular."

"But now you have 'You the man.'" I said. "It must make you proud to know that it's spread across the country."

I wondered if "You the man" was original or something he had heard somewhere else.

"You want the real truth?"

I nodded.

He said, "This crazy woman yelled it at me in a courtroom one day when I was bein' tried for a case of mistaken identity. I just took it to golf."

I had a suggestion for him. Something I thought might be good for the game. I said he should leave the PGA Tour for a while and start going to LPGA tournaments. He could also become the first person to yell, "You the woman!"

"Equal rights," I said with a shrug.

I left him staring at me peculiarly. Maybe he was mulling it over.

Be Happy
with Second Place

THERE IS a widely held belief among golfers who finish second in tournaments that they are tragic victims and have been swindled by the law firm of Destiny, Fate & Luck.

This is sometimes true, of course. As someone who has spent a lifetime finishing second in my own meager circles of competition—from various local amateur tournaments in a squandered youth to various senior flights in these declining years—I can speak with some authority on the subject.

Without any doubt, it is God's work.

You simply have to learn to live with it and understand the following rules:

1. If your car starts in cold weather, you'll finish second.

2. If your household air-conditioning works in hot weather, you'll finish second.

3. If all of your children are self-supporting and live in their own homes, you'll finish second, or worse.

You can't have it all.

And second place isn't so bad, after all. It means you could have been first. And runner-up is not such a bad word, once you get over the fact that it sounds like something the dry cleaner did to your cashmere sweater.

The words "second" and "runner-up" have always received very bad press, of course. They are associated with "loser." They call to mind silver, as in silver medal, which in most cultures is not as valuable as gold, although it is better than bronze, and certainly better than pewter, not to mention rust.

I remember this day when I was sitting around with Arnold Palmer in his den in Latrobe, Pennsylvania. I was admiring the coffee table that had been inlaid with the scads of gold medals he had won here and there. Among them, I noticed, were three silver medals. They were the ones Arnold had collected after losing three U.S. Open playoffs.

"What are these silver medals doing in here?" I asked.

He struggled momentarily for an explanation. "Uh, well . . . they, uh . . . aren't bad-looking."

I knew why the silver medals were in the table. They were reminders to Arnold that he might have won three more majors if it hadn't been for the ruthless law firm of Destiny, Fate & Luck.

You can gain new respect for the golfer who finishes second, the downtrodden runner-up, if you take a stroll with the immortals through the history of major championships. It's a silver mine.

Consider Jack Nicklaus. Everybody on this side of the Balkans is aware that Jack owns twenty majors, but it's often overlooked that he's been a runner-up nineteen times.

Yes, count them. He's been second in four U.S. Opens, four Masters Tournaments, four PGAs, and *seven* British Opens. To think that Nicklaus could have won 39 majors is a head-swimming mind-boggler, to say the least.

In this category of first or second in majors, there is nobody even close to Nicklaus. Here are the top 15 on the all-time gold-silver list:

PLAYER	1st	2nd	Total
Jack Nicklaus	20	19	39
Bobby Jones	13	6	19
Arnold Palmer	8	10	18
Ben Hogan	10	6	16
Gary Player	9	6	15
Tom Watson	8	7	15
Sam Snead	7	8	15
Walter Hagen	11	3	14
Harry Vardon	7	6	13
J. H. Taylor	5	7	12
Gene Sarazen	7	4	11
Byron Nelson	5	6	11
Lee Trevino	6	2	8
Raymond Floyd	4	4	8
Tom Morris, Sr.	4	4	8

Look closely and you will see that some gentlemen accumulated more silver than gold, but this doesn't mean that Palmer, Snead, Nelson, and Taylor were bad people. Rather, it is testimony to how often they were, as they say, *there.*

Snead's total doesn't take into account, for instance, the disastrous 8 he made on the 72nd hole at Spring

Mill in the 1939 U.S. Open when a par would have won and a bogey would have tied. He wound up fifth, two shots out.

Mere threads stood between Byron Nelson and four other majors. He lost by a single stroke after a 36-hole playoff in the 1946 U.S. Open and dropped three PGA finals—to lesser talents—on the 36th, 37th, and 38th holes.

Throughout the 1930s, a long-hitting fellow named Craig Wood suffered more agony than anyone. He lost so many big titles that "runner-up" became his nickname. People didn't say hello to Craig, they said, "Always a bridesmaid," quoting the wire-service wordsmiths.

Wood was the first man to score the Grand Slum or the Grand Slap, whichever way you wish to put it, by losing playoffs for all four majors. Like this:

1933: Lost playoff to Denny Shute for British Open.

1934: Lost playoff to Paul Runyan for PGA.

1935: Lost playoff to Gene Sarazen for Masters.

1939: Lost playoff to Byron Nelson for U.S. Open.

"It seems I'm destined never to win a big tournament," he often moaned.

Then came 1941, the year Wood captured both the Masters and the U.S. Open, which eased some of the pain.

To date, only one player has managed to duplicate Craig Wood's feat of scoring the Grand Slum/Grand Slap. That's the crowd-pleasing Australian, Greg Norman. Like this:?

1984: Lost playoff to Fuzzy Zoeller for U.S. Open.

1987: Lost playoff to Larry Mize for Masters.

1989: Lost playoff to Mark Calcavecchia for British Open.

1993: Lost playoff to Paul Azinger for PGA.

Actually, by my standards, to be an all-time silver king, you can't have ever won a gold—never a major. There is a four-way tie in this department. The 0-for-4 Award is shared by Macdonald Smith, Harry Cooper, Doug Sanders, and Bruce Crampton, although Crampton's name needs an asterisk—he was runner-up all four times to Jack Nicklaus.

Which means, of course, that neither God nor the swindling law firm had anything to do with it.

Saving the World

THIS GUY named Joe Slicer hadn't been seen around our club since he hit a tee shot over the condos on the eighteenth hole, threw his Mizuno in the lagoon, sold his furniture company, left his wife and kids, and went off to join the Agency.

Now he was back in town and I ran into him in the Men's Grill as he was eavesdropping on two members who were talking about the lie angle, shaft length, grip size, and swing weight of their new Ping Zing irons.

I asked Joe how he liked working undercover these days.

He said, "I had to do something to save my life. I was an addict. And I have to tell you that becoming a garc is the best thing that ever happened to me.

A garc?

"That's what they call us," he said. "I think it's somewhat derisive, frankly, but I'm proud to be a part of the GEA."

I said I hoped he wasn't here to bust *me*.

"No, you're okay. You only play on weekends. You only

have one set of clubs. It's the others I'm after—the real sickies."

Like who?

"The men whose entire lives are obsessed by golf. Golf is worse than drugs."

I could tell by Joe's expression that he believed this.

He said, "Golf causes emotional instability. It infiltrates areas where it doesn't belong. You remember how I used to be, don't you? In my patio home? How all of my door handles were made out of putter heads?"

I did remember that, but I only thought it made him silly, not ill.

"The Golf Enforcement Agency is going to save America," he said. "Golf is becoming far too excessive for too many people. The addicted golfer can't possibly deal with business or sexual issues."

He nodded at someone. "Look at Frank over there. All those logos on his shirt and cap. Do you know how much golf equipment he has in his home?"

I said I'd never been invited into Frank's home.

"Of course you haven't. There's no place to *sit*. That's why he's had four wives. His house is full of putting devices and driving nets. Golf has made him a serious victim of personality immaturity. He needs to do time."

Where?

"We have a golf correctional facility in Frozen Dog, Alaska. No golf there, boy."

I asked Joe what he thought was the cause of someone's golf addiction.

"Very simple," he said. "Golf is not a sport, it's a skill. But it's a skill with which almost anyone can accidentally hit a shot as well as Jack Nicklaus. And it only takes that *one shot* to give the person an adrenaline high that no other drug can equal."

I said I sort of understood that. I distinctly remembered the day Joe hit a 3-iron about two feet from the pin on the sixth hole even though he had been allowing for a 100-yard slice and was aiming at the chimney on my town house.

"Exactly," he said. "And I can tell you it was that very shot that instilled in me a denial mechanism that caused me to avoid all future business and marital problems."

I didn't quite get that.

"Don't question me on this," he said. "I've been through the training program at the GEA. Golf is definitely used to regulate a person's emotional life, to falsely help him achieve a sense of well-being. Control one golf shot and it stands to reason that the game can take on more significance than merely being a recreational outlet."

It was easy to notice that the GEA had given Joe a lot of new words. Once, he had mostly said things like 'That's right, bitch, hook some more!"

I asked about remedies. What could those of us do who enjoyed the game and wanted to keep playing it but didn't want to become an addict and wind up in Frozen Dog, Alaska?

The garc listed the following things:

1. Don't play more than twice a week.

2. Never own more than two sets of clubs or three putters.

3. Never sneak in nine after work.

4. Never bet more than your take-home pay.

5. Only read instruction books for the humor in them.

6. Only enter member-guest tournaments to entertain clients, and *never* expect to win anything.

7. Report immediately to the GEA anyone you know who buys a Stroke Master and slips it on his driver to measure club-head speed or buys a Swing-Trac slice-cure system.

8. If all else fails, revert to cigarettes and alcohol.

The World of Golf on Cable TV

WELCOME to another edition of *Gooney's Golf* here on Channel 73. I'm Duck Slice Gooney, your genial host, here to handle all your golfing needs on cable TV.

Ed, you want to tilt that camera up a little and get it on my face? Thank you, pard.

So here we are. Now you just sit back and relax for the next thirty minutes. I've got tips for you. I've got the latest in equipment for you. I've got a special guest for you tonight, a man who's gonna tell you a lot of things you don't know about froghair. And, of course, we'll be taking your call-ins. Dang, I see my phone's already ringing.

Hello. Duck Slice Gooney here. What can I do for your backswing?

"I'm Myrtle Sampson." Nice to hear from you, Myrtle. What's your question?

"I want to know how a fool like you got on my TV set."

Heh, heh. Which one of my golf buddies put you up to this, Myrtle? I bet it was old Sprinkler Head Murphy. Tell the truth.

"I don't know anybody named Murphy and I sure don't want to know *you*."

Do you play golf, Myrtle?

"No, I do not play golf. I hate golf."

Sorry to hear that, Myrtle.

"You would hate golf, too, if you were married for twenty-seven years to a worthless scum who played a lot more golf than he sold carpet! Goodbye."

Heh, heh. Well, there you go. Not everybody loves this game as much as the rest of us.

Modene! You want to screen them calls before I get me another terrorist on the air? Thank you, darlin'.

Now then, folks. You may think what I've got in my hand is an ordinary umbrella. The fact is, it's the latest stroke saver I've come across. Yeah, it's an umbrella but look what else it can do for you.

You fold this out and it becomes a seat. You open this end and a ball drops out—you don't never need to lose one in the rough. You fold out this doodad and this thing clicks in and you got yourself a putter. Now you pull up on this and it's the perfect scoop to fish your Ultra out of the creek. But there's more.

Don't overlook this thing that flies out if you press this button right here. Out comes the old chipping club!

But I've saved the best for last. Up underneath here is a tin bowl, and if you throw this switch, the rod heats up, and you've got yourself a way to make popcorn on them slow rounds when you're stranded on the sixth tee! It's called the Golf-O-Dee-Light and I'm happy to say it's on sale right now at your nearest Mall-Mart.

Okay. Time to bring in my guest, none other than Mr. Froghair himself, Lonnie Don Striper, my old friend from Rock Hollow muny. Have a seat, Lonnie. What are you gonna tell us about the froghair tonight?

"I've found the secret."

All right! Lay it on us, pard.

"Stay off of it. The percentages of making a par are better if you just go ahead and hit the dern ball onto the green."

Some of us can't do that all the time, Lonnie. Heh, heh. What other advice you got?

"I've been thinking a lot about the 2-iron lately."

What about the 2-iron, Lon?

"It ain't worth squat, is what I've been thinking. I'm not saying it's the case with every golfer's set of clubs, but my 2-iron's got a smaller face on it than, say, my 5-iron. Noticed it last week. So I started looking around, and I'll be derned if I didn't find several other 2-irons in other bags that were the same size. I think there's something going on in the manufacturing business."

Oops, there's the phone again. Hello. Duck Slice Gooney here with all your golfing needs on cable TV.

"Duck, this is Roy."

Hey, Roy, how you doin'? Folks, this is Roy Snapper, my good golf buddy.

"I found your ball, Duck."

What ball is that?

"The one you claimed you didn't lose on the fifteenth hole yesterday. I knew it was in that bush all along. Me and Red Grip went out there and looked for it and there it was. We're comin' over to get our money back."

We'll talk about it later, Roy. I'm on the air.

"We're pretty sure you palmed that hole in one last week, too, when our backs was turned. Red's got his shotgun loaded. I'd say you're about twenty minutes away from adiós, muchacho."

Folks, we'll take a little break here.

Modene! You want to get me 911?

Things That Make You Hot

GOLF IS A GAME of annoyances. You would think it would be enough that I have to put up with my own hasty-lazy swing as well as all of the silly obstacles on a course—water, sand, wind, etc.—things that are obviously designed to keep me from truly enjoying a full eighteen holes.

You would think that, yes, if you were a clearheaded, reasonable individual—like me.

But no.

I look around today and I find all of these other things I have to endure, things which I will now list in no particular order of annoyance.

• **Shorts and anklets.** Shorts are for tennis or yard work. Anklets are for the LPGA. Do you like losing to a guy who wears shorts and anklets? For that matter, do you even like being in the same foursome where the other three guys are wearing shorts and anklets?

Don't you feel, deep down, just a little less certain about your gender?

I mean, what is there to say at the end of a round? May I buy you ladies a drink in the Mixed Grill? Something like that?

• **A man who knows his exact slope.** I don't know my slope. I will never know my slope. I don't even *want* to know my slope. I don't even want to know what a slope *is*.

• **Advertising on tee markers.** I can say, quite honestly, that it has never helped me get a drive in the fairway in a member-guest when I learn from a glance that the fifth hole is brought to me by River City Warehouse & Storage, or that the fourteenth hole is brought to me by the Sunshine Bank Mortgage Loan Department.

• **Amusing head covers.** Let's see, Ed. I guess that funny-looking alligator on your driver means you're a Florida Gator, right?

Roy, there's no mistaking your Bertha for a big old furry Clemson Tiger, is there?

Notre Dame, huh, Fred? Nice leprechaun.

• **Absentminded cart drivers.** Well, there he goes again. He's parked it way over there on the right side of the green, even though it's fairly obvious that the next tee is through those trees on the left.

Okay, he's put the flag back in. Now he's found his putter. Good.

Oops, almost forgot the wedge. Yep. There it is, over by the bunker.

That's good. Go back and get the towel you never use. Don't walk too fast. Nobody's out here but *you*.

There you go. Circle back around. That's it—back

across the fairway in front of the green. Keep going, keep going.

Fine. Swell. Wonderful.

May *I* try to hit to the green now?

THANK YOU!

• **Plumb-bobbers.** My suspicion is, the vast majority of plumb-bobbers don't have any earthly idea what they're doing. But they've seen touring pros doing it, so they think *they* should do it.

I can tell the plumb-bobber what he's looking at. He's looking at those condos over there on the other side of the lagoon behind the green.

It is Harvey Penick who has the best question for plumb-bobbers.

How can a plumb bob tell you how hard to hit it?

• **The man who won't pick up when he's out of the hole.** What do you lie now, Ralph? Only seven? Great. I'll give you the bunker shot. Let's go. They made three.

• **The unsightly long putter.** This thing is stupid. It wobbles when you take it back. It wobbles even more when you bring it forward.

If you want to use it in the pole vault, fine.

But nobody ever sank a putt of any length with a long putter unless the ball accidentally hit two coins and a spike mark.

• **The 23-handicapper who goes out in 37.** He swears it's the luckiest nine he's ever played. He hates to think about how badly he's going to play on the back.

I know what he's going to shoot on the back. At the dead worst, a 39.

• **Individual iron covers.** Your wife knitted those? Really?

• **The man whose fun-loving nickname is proudly stitched into his huge leather bag.** In my day, I've been pitted against "The Hoss," "Old Pard," "The Stallion," "The Doctor," "Podna," "Side Bet," "Big Buck," "Cowboy Pete," and "Killer Bill," among others.

• **Cellular phone in the golf cart.** Frank will be with us in a minute. He's on his eighth phone call in the first three holes. His over-and-under number today is thirty for eighteen holes.

• **The old jokester.** Have I heard the one about the rabbi, the priest, and the lawyer who try to get on Augusta National and . . . ?

Yes!

Well, did I hear what Nicklaus said to St. Peter when . . . ?

YES!

Golf Nuts

LET'S TALK about golf nuts.

I'll start with the runty little sixty-eight-year-old combatant who always insists on playing from the gold tees.

He says you can't really *see* a golf course unless you play it from the tips.

He finds something terribly intriguing, as opposed to insane, about a 7,200-yard golf course, particularly if it's infested with water, waste, sand, bulkheads, trees, moguls, deep rough, violent wind, severe pins, and slick greens.

He would never improve a lie. He is greatly offended at the mere suggestion of a mulligan.

He loves playing a par-5 hole with driver, 3-wood, 5-wood, 7-wood, sand blast, pitch, chip, and four putts.

He is enthralled by a long, brutal par-4 hole that he can attack with driver, lateral, spoon, unplayable, 5-iron, boundary, 9-iron, cart path, pitch, and three putts.

He is fascinated with a killer par-3 hole that he can bring to its knees with driver, water, 5-wood, bulkhead, wedge, chip, and three putts.

One day he hopes to break 126.

"How did you play today, dear?" his wife asks.

"Great. I had a putt for a par and three chips at birdies."

Next, I give you the tireless gentleman who calls me every year or so to bring me up to date on the progress he's making in trying to play all of America's famous courses.

He has been at this for about twenty-five years, I guess.

In all of the phone calls over the past quarter of a century, he has asked me the same question.

Can I suggest anything that will help him get on Pine Valley, Augusta National, Merion, Seminole, Cypress Point, Oakmont, Los Angeles Country Club, Bel Air, Shinnecock Hills, Colonial, Winged Foot, Chicago Golf, Brook Hollow, or Olympic?

I used to say, "Crawl over the fence and don't play the first hole or the eighteenth."

Now I say, "Steal a hundred million dollars from your company and put a hyphen in your name."

I give you this retired fellow I've stumbled upon who plays six times a week and makes all of his own clubs. They are rather crude-looking things but he makes them in his workshop.

Although golf is obviously his life, he has been pleased to inform me that he has never attended a tournament, doesn't watch golf on TV, doesn't read golf books, doesn't read golf magazines, and doesn't even read the sports pages in newspapers.

One day he asked what I did for a living. I said I was a writer.

"What do you mean?" he said, looking at me as if he

had just heard of the most bizarre profession imaginable.

I said, well, among other things, I write articles for a golf magazine.

He looked at me for a long moment, and then said, "Why?"

I excused myself hurriedly and went home and reported to my wife that I thought I had just met the mysterious sniper who fires at motorists from a freeway overpass.

Also in my neighborhood is this elderly man who only plays on weekends but spends the rest of his time hunting golf balls.

He's always out there during the week, creeping through the trees or poking around at the edge of lagoons.

It is rumored that he has over 10,000 golf balls in his garage, where he keeps them neatly arranged on shelves.

More than one person has told me I *must* visit this man's garage—his collection of golf balls is astounding.

"It's on my list," I say nicely.

As amazing as anyone I've heard about lately is the dentist. He is said to be a lifelong fan of Arnold Palmer. He is said to be such a fan of Arnold's, it borders on mental illness.

I don't know if it's true—I can only hope—but the dentist is purported to carry in his pocket a ball marker made from the gold that was extracted from Arnold's teeth.

This might not make him the biggest Arnold Palmer fan in the world, however.

There was a journalist in Great Britain whose unbounding hero worship of Palmer became legend. He was never satisfied, one hears, with autographs, scrap-books, photos, paintings, or articles about Arnold.

One day he got the inspired idea to begin collecting the divots Palmer would take out of fairways in England and Scotland. Eventually, the entire lawn of his home near London was made out of Arnold Palmer divots.

Actually, if I were to follow through on a thought I had the other day, I think I could be exempt on the Golf Nut Tour myself.

You see, I have this habit of knocking balls into the woods when they betray me. I might add that it doesn't take much for me to feel betrayed. A four-foot putt that curls out, a pulled 7-wood that winds up in a bunker, a chip shot that races across the green and into the frog-hair, a tee shot that defies its stern warning and seeks out the forest.

I've been leaving these balls in the woods, but I've come up with a better idea. A small cemetery in my yard. It could be fenced in by a variety of broken shafts. Call me the Mortician.

In this cemetery I will bury all of the golf balls that betray me, because if they can betray me once, they will certainly betray me again. Planted into the earth, how-ever, they will have nothing to do but rot in eternal hell forever.

Never again will they be able to bring unwarranted grief and anguish to some innocent golfer, like myself, who never meant them any harm whatsoever.

It's what they deserve, I say. All I've ever asked of them is a simple string of bogeys.

Riding High

A HIGH-HANDICAPPER named Sigmund Freud once said it's useless to psychoanalyze people over the age of fifty—they are too set in their ways and are going to die soon anyhow. Freud said this, of course, before the advent of senior golf.

Freud's statement was first brought to my attention back during my college days. It happened in the coffee shop of the campus drugstore, where such lofty things were often discussed for eighteeen hours at a time, and I quickly took it to mean that after I reached the age of fifty I would no longer have to apologize for my unrequited love for golf carts.

From the time I first rode in a golf cart as a teenager, I have never seen one I didn't like, even the loud ones, even the three-wheelers.

But I think my position on motorized golf was well stated and made perfectly clear in my book *Tarmac Golf.* The major theme of the book was that I enjoyed golf carts as much as I enjoyed many other modern inventions, such as, to mention only five of the most obvious:

a. Fast-forward on the VCR.
b. Automobile air-conditioning.
c. Ice dispenser on the refrigerator.
d. Miniskirts.
e. Hit till you're happy.

For myself and other lovers of golf carts, however, there are two things today which annoy us greatly.

One is the 90-percent-cart rule. The other is the stay-completely-on-the-cart-path rule.

If you're observing the 90-percent-cart rule, you're supposed to stay on the tarmac until you reach your ball, then you may drive to it.

If you're observing the cart-path rule, you're not expected to leave the tarmac at all; you have to get out of the cart and walk to your ball in every instance, no matter how far away it may be hiding in the trees or weeds.

Both rules are utterly idiotic, and I never follow them, except on those rare occasions when the ranger wakes up from his nap and calls them to my attention.

Grass grows back. I've seen it happen time and again.

The virtues of riding for eighteen holes as opposed to walking for eighteen holes are so numerous I can't possibly cover them all in this space, but I will touch on a few.

In my experience, one of the major advantages is that you can sometimes drive to your snap hook and get there before the ball stops rolling. Walking can take days.

In the same sense, you can chase your sky-slice tee shot and sometimes reach it in time to make an outfielder's catch before it lands in the lagoon.

Driving means you can swerve around, or cruise past, joggers and power-walkers who have collapsed in flower beds from heart attacks. You don't have to step over them to get to your 7-wood shot.

The true cart lover, by the way, doesn't like to *share* a golf cart. It's too inconvenient—almost as inconvenient as walking.

If you hit a good long drive, for example, your cart companion is odds-on to hit a short crooked drive. And so on.

Besides that, if you're in a cart alone, nobody is going to try to sell you a computer, an insurance policy, or a ticket to a charity function, or comment on how many cigarettes you smoke.

The biggest advantage in riding alone, however, is how much it can improve your score.

In a reliable cart, you can hurriedly get to the ball in the rough and provide it with a better lie. In a reliable cart, you can get to the back of the green quickly and discover that your ball doesn't deserve to be in the bunker at all.

In a reliable cart, you can arrive at the green ahead of everyone else and test the break and speed of what might have been a particularly tricky putt.

And perhaps more important than anything, in a reliable cart, you can ascertain that your drive wasn't in a ditch or out-of-bounds, as the view from the tee box surely suggested.

A chapter in *Tarmac Golf* points out a curious thing. Young people like golf carts better than older people. This is basically because young people are very tired.

Surveys show that the average young person can sleep for twelve, fourteen, sixteen, twenty hours a day, whereas older people are lucky to sleep five hours a night, because of their dogs, which sleep in the bed with them, or their kidneys, which rarely sleep at all.

I have personally witnessed young people who were content to watch the Spanish channel on TV for half a day rather than crawl to a nearby piece of furniture to retrieve the remote clicker.

It is essentially daylight that makes young people so tired, and I seem to remember this from my own youth. Young people are, therefore, sitting ducks for golf carts.

The Luck of Calcutta Bob and Suntan Jim

IT'S TIME for the annual member-guest at our club, and it will be good to see old Calcutta Bob and Suntan Jim again—if they are still alive.

They made a big impression on a lot of us last year.

Darned if old Calcutta Bob didn't show up for the festive event and shoot 69 and 71 on his own ball despite his handicap of 18, and darned if old Suntan Jim didn't shoot 68 and 69 despite his handicap of 16. They won their tenth flight and the overall championship by 18 strokes.

It was a remarkable performance by a couple of high-handicappers, although some of the cynics around the club were impertinent enough to suggest that Calcutta Bob and Suntan Jim didn't love the game of golf as much as they loved silver trophies and the $25,000 in first-place calcutta money.

Calcutta Bob was an out-of-state member of the club.

Suntan Jim was his guest. But their handicaps were evidently honest, because they were certified by the head pro at Crime Spree Country Club in their hometown of Bird's Nest, South Carolina.

Calcutta Bob said it was the luckiest two days of golf he ever played in his whole life. Suntan Jim said it was the luckiest two days of golf he had ever played in his whole life.

Calcutta Bob and Suntan Jim got quite a bit of sympathy when they arrived at the club. Their pickup truck had a flat and they drove in on the rim.

Calcutta Bob was wearing a neck brace and confessed at the barbecue that he was also suffering from a rare heart disease. Coincidentally, Suntan Jim's right arm came out of the sling that very night.

It was easy enough for Calcutta Bob and Suntan Jim to buy themselves in the calcutta pool for only $50. I wasn't going to bid on them. I was too busy paying $400 for half of the team of two doctors, $300 for half of the team of two dentists, $200 for half of the team of two lawyers, and $250 for half of the team of two bankers.

Besides, I had played a practice round with Calcutta Bob and Suntan Jim. In the round, Calcutta Bob developed this severe hook off the tee and this severe shank with his irons. He shot 105. Meanwhile, Suntan Jim developed this wild slice off the tee and this top thing with his irons and he shot 113.

My carpet-salesman partner and me were paired with Calcutta Bob and Suntan Jim in the first round.

Calcutta Bob acted as surprised as me on the first tee when he had somehow misplaced his severe hook and drove the ball 280 yards down the middle. "How'd that happen?" he said.

Then Suntan Jim got up and drove 275 yards down

the middle, completely devoid of his wild slice. "Beats anything I ever saw," he apologized.

They kept apologizing all the way around the course. Calcutta Bob apologized with tears in his eyes after he hit a 1-iron 240 yards to a foot of the hole on a par 3 for a net 1.

"I'm really sorry," he said. "That ball should have kicked in the bunker."

Suntan Jim apologized with tears in his eyes after he reached the green in two with a driver and 3-iron on our 600-yard par 5. It was a little downwind, of course.

"I'll probably three-putt that 20-footer," he said, rolling in the triple-breaking downhiller for a net 2.

It was truly unfortunate that my partner and I were in the tough tenth flight. Not only was this the flight that featured Calcutta Bob and Suntan Jim but also the doctors, dentists, lawyers, and bankers.

I must say, however, that the doctors, dentists, lawyers, and bankers complained the loudest about Calcutta Bob and Suntan Jim.

The doctors, who play every day, had 13 and 14 strokes and shot 30 under for the two rounds, but they didn't come close to catching Calcutta Bob and Suntan Jim, who were 48 under for the 36 holes. The dentists, who play every day, had 13 and 15 strokes and they shot 24 under. The lawyers, who play every day and had 12 and 13 strokes, shot 21 under. The bankers, who play every day and had 11 and 13 strokes, shot 19 under.

I had 11 strokes and my partner had 9. We played our hearts out and even got a few breaks. We shot even par.

And I was reminded once again that the thing I like best about the member-guest tournaments is shooting your handicap and finishing last in your flight. It's part of the charm.

Debunking the Firm Left Side

YOU MAY RECALL that in my best-selling instruction book, *How to Play Relatively Good Golf While Thinking About Kim Basinger,* I was the first teacher to debunk the Firm Left Side Theory.

As I pointed out in the text, and as was vividly depicted in the watercolor illustrations that my ten-year-old daughter contributed, there is no such thing as a firm left side while swinging a club, particularly the driver.

Not unless, as I stated, the golfer has suffered a curious birth defect or is known to drink gin excessively.

Thus, the golfer is forced to make choices. He may have one of the following:

1. A firm left arm.
2. A firm left shoulder.
3. A firm left leg.
4. A firm left hip.

The golfer might also have any two of the above, but my tests proved conclusively that he could never have all of them at once. This is what inspired the chapter "Keep Your Shoulder Against the Wall," for it was the firm shoulder that I recommended ahead of the other choices.

Although I thought I made myself very clear that I was talking about the *left* shoulder, apparently some readers have misunderstood and thought I was talking about the right shoulder.

They have written to complain that by keeping their right shoulder against the imaginary wall, they have been unable to take the club back, except on the occasional chip shot.

Well, pardon *me* for assuming that I was addressing intelligent people.

Since my space is limited, let me move on to a few other things that have caused a certain amount of confusion.

In the chapter on golf gloves, "Hold on for Dear Life," in which I said that the glove should always be worn on the right hand. I, of course, did not mean that the glove, literally, should be worn on the *right* hand.

I mean, gimme a break here. What did you think when you put the glove on your right hand and your little finger slid into the thumb hole?

The glove naturally should be worn on the left hand, which is what I meant when I cautioned you to be sure the glove was on the right hand.

As for my suggesting that it is perfectly acceptable to spit in a new glove, to enhance the grip, I thought I underlined the fact that you should spit IN YOUR OWN GLOVE, NOT SOMEONE ELSE'S.

I'm sorry if this well-intended advice has caused some altercations for a few of you.

Now for the business about the mind. The subject seems to intrigue many readers. I can only refer you again to "The Ball Is the Enemy," my chapter on anger.

If you will consult the illustrations again, you will see a golfer envisioning the ball to be (1) a fat Iraqi, (2) a banker rejecting your loan application, or (3) an IRS auditor.

As I suggest, you should imagine the golf ball to be any of these three characters at address, particularly on a tight driving hole with out-of-bounds looming on one side of the fairway or the other.

You *do not* want to hit the Iraqi, the banker, or the IRS auditor out-of-bounds, for this obviously means he will get away unharmed. The idea is to keep him *in-bounds* to be able to punish him severely with all of the other clubs in your bag as you complete the hole.

As anger becomes a part of your game, *don't worry about appearance*. At times, you are most definitely going to find yourself hitting *down* on the ball with a snarling vengeance, and hitting *up* on the ball with a slobbering relish.

It is even possible to hit *down* and *up* on the ball in the same swing, as in the bunker shot, which some of you may have discovered by now.

With anger as a positive force in your game, you are going to find yourself hitting the ball straighter and far greater distances, but if progress seems to be coming too slowly, you may need to discard the Iraqi, the banker, and the IRS auditor, and conjure up new images.

A long list is provided in my book, such as a lawyer, a

TV repairman, an arrogant maître d', a tailgating motorist, and a golf writer, to name only a few possibilities.

It goes without saying, although I did not by any means let it go without saying it in my book, that the mind can play an even more important role on the greens. I can only beg you to reread "Get Over It," my chapter on putting. The crucial tip in this chapter, I think, is to envision the cup as an enormous, bottomless pit and the ball as an ex-wife you never want to hear from again.

Works for me.

What Is This Lost-Ball Business?

THE RULES OF GOLF are dumb. Granted, this statement comes from a man whose backswing today is restricted by a stomach that has devoted much of its life to storing up sausage, biscuits, and gravy, but I've always said the same thing—the Rules of Golf are dumber than carrots.

Like here I am, let's say, more than 400 yards away from a little hole in the ground and I'm supposed to get there in four strokes even though I have to fight the wind, go around trees, over water, through sand, and out of weeds, armed only with my chronic draw-fade tee ball.

Don't I have enough problems?

No. My ball also rests in a fairway divot, which *I* didn't create. And three agents of the FBI are glaring at me, pistols drawn, waiting for me to make a false move.

And why? Because a long time ago a bunch of guys

in coats and ties and funny accents drank a vat of brandy and made up these *rules* that only Ben Hogan could live by.

That day, Sir Rodney turned to Sir James and said, "I rather think the game needs some rules, don't you?"

"I do, rather," said Sir James.

"Let's make them rather impossible."

"By all means. Rather oblique, if I have a say about it."

"Here, here," said Sir Trevor, joining in. "Stickier the better for my money. We wouldn't want the game to be so easy that any lout could shoot in the 80s, would we?"

Then they went ahead and made up all these rules about where did the ball cross the cliff before it disappeared into the canyon, lifting illegal twigs, accidentally stepping on your ball in the rough, animals that either burrow or do not, grounding your club in a swamp, and so forth.

Take the rule about teeing off. They have got these markers you are supposed to stand between or the FBI agents will plug you in the chest.

Like I am at this 217-yard par 3 over a lake and it's going to make a *big difference* if I tee up my ball a yard in front of the markers. Yeah, sure. My 3-wood has been known to hole out a lot of shots from 216 yards, right?

Dumb.

Take this thing about boundaries. Like I'm in the woods off the tee but there's this white stake that says I'm out-of-bounds, although there's nothing but more trees on the other side of the white stake.

It's not like my ball is sitting in somebody's eggs Benedict. And what difference should *that* make? I've got an eggs Benedict shot. The trick is to hit the ball before you hit the poached egg, the Canadian bacon, or the muffin. And why is the guy eating outdoors on his condo patio anyhow?

Take this marking-your-ball-on-the-green thing. I'm 45 feet from the cup but the FBI agents are watching closely to make sure I don't mark my ball with a discus, leaving myself only 44½ feet from the cup.

Of course they are. I'm famous for my talent of sinking 44½-foot putts for pars and bogeys, right?

I mean, *come on.* I get a penalty because my ball decides to hide in a shrub and not let anybody find it?

I'm already out $2.66 and I suffer a penalty, too.

Hey ruleswad! Get real, okay?

You can trace my attitude about golf rules back to when I was a kid, playing in my first kids' tournament in Texas. There was this hole where I found my tee ball up against a root in the rough.

I bent over to lift the root away from my ball, but the root didn't want to be picked up right away. Well, I didn't have to take that from a root—and I wasn't about to swing at the root and ball at the same time. Break a shaft? Fracture my wrist? What for?

I tugged on the root. Long enough to plow up about six feet of dirt, rocks, wildflowers. Long enough to discover that the root more or less ran from Fort Worth to Waco.

In the meantime, my ball rolled three or four inches, and my opponent was staring at me.

"Your ball moved," he said.

"So what?" I said.

"That's a penalty," he said.

He was a junior G-man.

"Why is it a penalty?" I said. "I didn't swing at it. Besides, the way it looks from here, I'm still behind eight trees, a creek, and four bunkers."

"I'm pretty sure it's a penalty."

"Where'd your drive go?"

"Aw, I'm over there in the water."

"Tell you what. You don't count the root, I don't count the water."

"Good deal," he said, grinning.

We played the rest of the match by my rules, and with seven or eight mulligans apiece we both broke 80.

I guess you could say I was lucky to win when I sank that 44½-foot putt on the last green.

Ever since then, I've always said golf was more fun if there was fairness involved.

The Perfect Driver

BEING A MAN of action, I finally got fed up one day with watching stooped-over, wheezing, seventy-three-year-old golfers outhit me off the tee simply because they had better equipment than I did. That's when I started my quest for the perfect driver.

I already owned a stockpile of twenty drivers, but most of them had been purchased for accuracy. I might add that a great many of these drivers did not furnish any accuracy, which is why they had wound up in my golf museum, or, as my wife would refer to it, our carport.

In any case, it was time to solve this length problem. If I could find the perfect driver, made of space-age materials that would frighten an extraterrestrial, I was absolutely convinced that I'd no longer have to witness a stooped-over, wheezing, seventy-three-year-old man outdrive me by 20 to 40 yards, after which I'd have to help him climb back into the golf cart and assist with his medication.

First, I decided to buy a PowerClout Widebody

Launcher. This was the club Frank Simcox was using the last time he airmailed me all day long. Frank is the stooped-over, wheezing, seventy-three-year-old who lives in the condo next to ours.

I apologized to my wife for the fact that the PowerClout Widebody Launcher was so expensive. It cost $2,367, primarily because it is constructed of Flutorium-X, a rare metal found only in the volcanoes near Bali, and blended with the lining of killer whales.

My wife, Martha, didn't mind the expense. She is an understanding person. She said, "You have to do what you have to do, dear," as she made plans to recarpet our entire home.

At first, the PowerClout Widebody Launcher added at least six yards to my overall distance, but this was before it seemed to lose interest in my swing and started hitting dribble-doppers.

That's when I started admiring Ralph Waynegrab's new driver. Ralph is my stooped-over, wheezing, seventy-three-year-old friend who lives in one of those pink patio homes along the twelfth fairway, across from the pond where the alligators hold their seminars.

Ralph had been outhitting me about 30 yards on the average with his Hefty Hog, which, as you know, was the first of the metal driving clubs. Now, suddenly, he was flying it 50 to 60 yards beyond my best lick with his 9-degree SuperMass FrequencyImpact Big Bouncer.

The Big Bouncer had a head on it the size of an astronaut's helmet, and the sound it made when it struck the ball was similar to that of five hubcaps being dropped on a marble porch from a second-story window.

I was impressed and went straight to Red Burdine, our director of golf, to inquire about the Big Bouncer.

Red Burdine confided that the Big Bouncer achieved

incredible distance because it was constructed out of Tatranium-Z, a metal that could only be found in sunken Japanese aircraft carriers near Midway and was blended with particles of dirt collected from underground nuclear tests near Smolensk. These were the reasons why the Big Bouncer would cost $5,489.22, less Red's usual $10 discount because he was my good friend.

"The Big Bouncer is the answer for you," he said. "It has the vertical axis to control your launch angle."

Naturally. I thought it best to discuss this expenditure with Martha over breakfast.

She read some of the front-page stories in the newspaper to me first. Something about four million people killing each other in the Balkans.

"I'd like to talk about something important," I said. "I don't have a sufficient thickness in the face of my PowerClout. I need to buy a Big Bouncer."

"Well, I think you should have one, dear," she said, smiling.

"I'm glad you agree," I said. "The Big Bouncer will give me those gravity influences I've been lacking, particularly on the long par 5s."

Martha said, "We should go get you one right now. We can ride over in my new Cadillac."

I'm sure the Big Bouncer would have given me the distance I wanted if I had ever been able to get the ball in the air with it, but of course it went into the museum in less than two weeks.

That's why I was so happy to see the driver that Roy Fitzhugh was using. Roy is my stooped-over, wheezing, seventy-three-year-old friend who lives in those orange town houses by the eighth fairway. He can hardly get the club back and his follow-through is more like a lunge, but he could bust it 80 or 90 yards past me with that odd-looking club that didn't even have a name.

I'm trying to find one now. Roy told me it was made of something called persimmon.

Hap McWedge and the Senior Amateurs

IT SEEMS that while my very back was turned a thing called senior amateur golf has become huge, as in mammoth, bordering on enormous. Every club apparently has one today—that fellow in his declining years who has given up life for golf, who now traipses all around the country to compete in such events as the coveted Hap McWedge Society of Seniors Invitational.

I know a lot of these gentlemen. They used to iron me out in high school and collegiate competition. Today, they're serving on USGA committees, Southern regional rules committees, Eastern regional turf management committees, Midwestern regional slow-play committttees, Mid-Southeastern course-rating committees, and various local snack-bar committees.

They haven't missed a round of golf in forty years, even during floods and tornadoes, and they play better golf now than they ever did, thanks to the nuclear shaft and hydrogen ball.

Most haven't shot above 74 from the blues since the winter of '67, which was the last time they spoke to their wives on a subject other than golf.

These fine players don't get the publicity they deserve, so I thought I'd give you a few of their bios.

Hap McWedge

Lovable founder of the Western Society of Seniors organization and five-time winner of the Hap McWedge Society of Seniors Invitational, a tournament with a format so complicated only Hap himself can explain it. At the age of sixty-seven, his three hip replacements haven't hindered his distance off the tee. Sold his ready-mix concrete business when he was twenty-seven years old and hasn't worked a day since. Only a year ago, Hap shot a final-round 68 at Long Grape, the new 8,000-yard par-70 Pete Dye course in Napa, California.

Dr. Fred Overlap

A seventeen-time winner of the National Ear, Nose & Throat Open, Dr. Fred currently limits his medical practice to two hours a week, between 6 and 8 A.M. on Mondays. At seventy-two years of age, his game continues to improve despite two hip replacements and a quadruple bypass. Presently organizing the Super Vintage Seniors Tour for golfers over the age of seventy with handicaps of no worse than 3. Only a year ago, Dr. Fred shot a final-round 67 to win the Senior Legends at Dripping Bunkers, the new 8,500-yard par-70 Pete Dye course near Victoria Falls, Zimbabwe. A methodical player, rarely smiles.

Brig. Gen. E. R. Grimes (Ret.)

Fondly known to his fellow competitors as "Mr. Rules" and "Time Control." Three hip replacements, two bypasses. The general's call-ins after observing rules violations on telecasts have resulted in seven disqualifications, to date, on the PGA Tour. Carries a stopwatch. Once disqualified the entire field for slow play in a Missouri Senior event, scoring his only victory. Shot a 69 at Pitching Deck, the new 9,000-yard par-70 Pete Dye course on board the USS *Saratoga*.

Walter (Waddy) Yammer

Lovable, fun-loving founder of the North-Central Texas Senior Golf Association, and the popular Waddy Yammer Partnership Alternate-Shot Modified Pinehurst-Vegas Senior Scramble. A keen historian, Waddy also makes his own antique clubs. Both of his daughters, Prestwick and Troon, are avid golfers. Introduced timeshare castles to his many Scottish friends. Recently announced that his tournament will be moving from its original site, Gullane No. 4, the nine-hole course he designed himself around his used-car lot in Waco, Texas, to a layout that can accommodate a larger field. Waddy has chosen Bent Wind, the new 10,000-yard par-70 Pete Dye course that uniquely blends sections of state farm roads with barbed-wire fences on the Four Deuces Ranch. Although winless on the senior amateur circuit, primarily because of the five hip replacements that force him to putt from a folding chair, Waddy is nonetheless a fixture at most prize-giving ceremonies, where he frequently seizes the mike to read his epic one-hour poem "Ode to the Beardies," which was inspired by his trip to Scotland in 1971.

Smokey Joe Wooten

Winner of more senior amateur events than any other current player. Regained his amateur status after forty years as a touring pro, teaching pro, and director of golf in the Carolinas. Longest hitter among seniors for two reasons. One, Smokey Joe is 6-foot-5, weighs 250 pounds. Two, his driver. It is a homemade copy of Big Bertha with a 57-inch shaft. Travels in an RV with his wife, Jody, and his pet rooster, Ben Byron Sam. The RV has amusing personalized license plate: "U-R 4-DOWN." Carries only ten clubs—driver, 3-wood, 1-iron, putter, and six wedges. Last year, Smokey Joe competed in thirty-five senior events, winning sixteen. Caused a sensation by firing a final-round 63 in the Unindicted CEO Seniors at Splash-O-Links, the new 11,000-yard par-70 Pete Dye course built on a series of offshore drilling rigs near Coon Point, Louisiana.

The Most Dangerous Job in Golf

THE TOURING PRO likes to think he has a tough life, living on the whim of his putting stroke from week to week, but as I have observed the game over the past 4,000 years, it is the country club professional who has the most dangerous job in golf—his life expectancy is more or less equal to that of a goldfish.

Every time I hear a club pro brag that he has the best job in the business, at one of the finest clubs in America, I find out six months later that he's been fired and was even forced to leave town urgently to avoid physical harm.

The recent case of Sweater Bob Shafter at the Peach Farm Country Club illustrates my point.

Sweater Bob was a respected teacher, a marketing genius, a public relations whiz. All of Sweater Bob's colleagues agreed on this, and so did Sweater Bob. Sweater Bob was also certain that he was beloved around Peach

Farm, for like any astute club pro, he had sought out the most influential members in the club and seemed to get along with them exceedingly well.

The influential members at Peach Farm included several of the most powerful businessmen in America. Augusta, Pine Valley, Cypress Point, they all had strong members, but Sweater Bob arrogantly said they couldn't match Peach Farm's lineup of CEO Smith, Sr., CEO Smith, Jr., Chuck Developer, Wiley Banker, Tom Leverage, Judge Hangum, Ed Savings, and Bob Loan, to name only a few.

"Stronger than an Ultra on a downhill chip," as Sweater Bob liked to put it, being witty.

Sweater Bob was the envy of all the club pros in the country for about a year, as I recall. But then that mysterious thing happened, as it happens to all club pros.

Sweater Bob was in his shop one morning alone, drinking a cup of coffee, when Ed Savings came in.

"Why aren't you selling something?" Ed Savings asked, and Sweater Bob noted irritation in the member's voice.

"There's nobody in here," Sweater Bob said innocently.

"I don't see that as much of an excuse," said Ed Savings.

"You're absolutely right," Sweater Bob said. "I think I'll buy a purple slipover for myself."

"What size?" said Ed Savings.

"XL," Sweater Bob said. "As a matter of fact, I'll take a red one, too."

"That's more like it," Ed Savings said, and walked away.

Thirty minutes later, Bob Loan came in, looking troubled.

"Good morning, Bob," Sweater Bob said cheerfully.

"What did you call me?"

"I meant Mr. Loan," the club pro replied apologetically.

"You know those irons you sold me last week?"

"Yes, sir."

Bob Loan said, "The 2- and 3-irons hook, the 4 and 5 top everything, the 6 and 7 shank, and the 8 and 9 go clickity off to the right. I'm going to play eighteen more holes with these irons today, but if I get the same results, I wouldn't want to assess your future around here."

It was an hour later that Wiley Banker came in, having just played nine holes. "Who set the pin on number three?" he said.

"I'm not sure," Sweater Bob said.

"I'll tell you who it was," Wiley Banker said. "It was an idiot who hates golf. The pin was front left, right next to the water. Do I look like I'm wearing an Aqua-lung?"

As Wiley Banker stormed out, CEO Smith, Sr., and CEO Smith, Jr., came in off the course with Judge Hangum. CEO Smith, Sr., looked deeply disturbed and was clenching his fist. To Sweater Bob, he said, "I'd like for you to explain this!"

CEO Smith, Sr., opened his fist. He was holding a filter-tipped cigarette butt. A wave of nausea swept over Sweater Bob.

"This was in the fourteenth fairway," CEO Smith, Sr., snarled.

"It was?" said Sweater Bob.

"Are you questioning me?"

"Are you questioning my father?" said the chinless CEO Smith, Jr.

"No, sir," Sweater Bob whimpered. "If you say it was

there, I'm sure it was there, but I can't believe a member would do such a thing."

"Are you accusing a member?"

"On second thought, no," Sweater Bob said. "It's probably mine, although I don't smoke."

"Just as I suspected," said the old man. With that, knowing it would be ruled justifiable homicide by Judge Hangum, who had ridden once too often in one of Sweater Bob's slow carts, CEO Smith, Sr., pulled out a gun and fired three shots into Sweater Bob's chest. Sweater Bob staggered and CEO Smith, Jr., caught him as he sank to the floor.

It was a comfort to the club pro's wife and family that he died as he had lived—in the arms of a rich man.

PART TWO

Order the Nostalgia
and Tell Them Heavy
on the Hogan

Hogan

EVER SINCE I was a kid and heard it "live" on the radio, and read about it in the newspaper, and saw it happen in a newsreel at the Hollywood Theater in Fort Worth, I've vigorously contended that Ben Hogan, my idol from the same hometown, won his first National Open in June of 1942, even though it came at a time when I couldn't find a Hershey bar anywhere because America and chocolate had gone to war.

This feat of Ben's, of course, has turned out to be terribly inconvenient for certain historians, inasmuch as it gives Hogan five Opens instead of four, or one more than Bobby Jones and Jack Nicklaus, not to forget Willie Anderson, who used to bring the monsters to their knees with rounds of 81.

Okay, that championship in '42 wasn't formally called the U.S. Open—it was the Hale America National Open Golf Tournament.

Okay, it wasn't played at Interlachen in Minneapolis, where the '42 Open was originally scheduled—it was played at the Ridgemoor Country Club in Chicago. Interlachen backed out as the host club a few months after Pearl Harbor, basically, I assume, because many of its potential gallery marshals and rough-growers had gone off to fight Germans and Japs.

Okay, the championship wasn't run exclusively by the blue coats and armbands—it was only *co-sponsored* by the U.S. Golf Association, along with the PGA of America and the Chicago District Golf Association.

Okay, the proceeds at the Ridgemoor didn't go to the USGA to invest in turf experiments—they went to benefit the United Service Organizations and the Navy Relief Fund.

And, okay, Ridgemoor was not as properly manicured as the normal Open course, which is to say that with the war on, the late Joe Dey didn't have the work force to grow the rough up to everybody's knees, shave the greens down to marble, and reduce Ridgemoor's par from 72 to 70.

But to all of those things I have always said: so what?

It behooves me to remind everyone that they played a "wartime" Masters in April that year, which Byron Nelson won, and historians count it. They played a "wartime" PGA in May that year, which Sam Snead won at Seaview in Atlantic City, and historians count it.

So what's wrong with counting the only National Open that was played in '42, particularly since it was won by Ben Hogan and not by Joe Zilch?

I've never had a problem putting Ben's victory at Ridgemoor in 1942 in the same lofty category with his great triumphs at Riviera in '48, Merion in '50, Oakland Hills in '51, and Oakmont in '53.

I might add—for whatever sentimental value it might have—that Ben didn't use to have a problem with this either.

There was this day, I recall, when Ben returned to Colonial Country Club in Fort Worth after winning at Merion in '50. Somebody said, "Congratulations on your second Open, Ben."

"Third," Ben responded quietly as he walked away.

There was this day at Colonial when Ben returned from winning at Oakland Hills in '51. Somebody said, "Congratulations on your third Open, Ben."

"Fourth," he said, smiling, going about his business.

Not to imply that Hogan ever went around campaigning for a fifth Open. Ben does consider that he won a *major* at Ridgemoor.

Well, look. Hogan has these *five* gold medals, see? They still highlight the Ben Hogan Trophy Room at Colonial, and all five medals look exactly the same, like the kind of medal they give you when you win a U.S. Open championship.

I say a man who owns five gold medals for winning U.S. Opens has won five U.S. Opens.

One day I delved into the newspaper microfilms to refresh my memory and strengthen my argument about that championship in 1942.

It seems that a record 1,540 golfers entered local qualifying at sixty-nine sites around the country. It also seems that sectional qualifying was held in Toronto, Boston, Chicago, Kansas City, Denver, Bloomfield, New Jersey; Atlanta, Detroit, Minneapolis, Buffalo, Cincinnati, Tulsa, Dallas, and Los Angeles.

I ask you: What were they doing holding nationwide qualifying tournaments if there wasn't going to be something similar to a U.S. Open at Ridgemoor Country Club in mid-June of '42?

Here's a paragraph from the Associated Press report of the opening rounds:

"There was a furor of excitement in the locker rooms when officials of the United States Golf Association ruled that the irons of Sam Byrd of Ardmore, Pa., were too deeply scored and that he could not use them."

I ask you this: What was the USGA doing inspecting grooves—or ruling on anything else—if this was not a U.S. Open?

This championship unfolded the way most U.S. Opens do. Otey Crisman, a "little-known pro from Alabama," tied Mike Turnesa for the first-round lead. Turnesa held the 36-hole lead by three strokes over Hogan, who shot a 62 in the second round. Hogan moved into a 54-hole tie with Turnesa at 203, as Jimmy Demaret became a strong contender, only two shots back.

With only four holes to play in the final round, Demaret led by two strokes, but Hogan played the last four holes in two under for a closing 68 and a 72-hole total of 271, while Demaret played the last four holes in three over and wound up tied with Turnesa for second.

"HALE AMERICA IS FIRST MAJOR TITLE FOR TEXAS BEN."

That was the headline in the Fort Worth *Star-Telegram*.

The lead on the AP report of June 22, 1942, reads:

"CHICAGO, June 21 — Tiny Ben Hogan, never before a winner in a major golf tournament, crashed to a dramatic victory in the Hale America National Open Sunday with a 72-hole total of 271, 17 under par for the distance.

"The 29-year-old Texan stood off a late challenge by colorful Jimmy Demaret. Demaret led Hogan by two strokes through 68 holes, but Hogan, refusing to blow up under pressure, picked up five strokes on the last four holes to triumph."

I have only one last thing to ask: If that wasn't a U.S. Open in '42, how come Hogan won it?

I bring up all this business about a "fifth Open" only as a preamble for a golfing performance that seems, frankly, as if it happened only yesterday to those of us who were lucky enough to see parts of it and who manage to live quite comfortably in the past, thank you.

I speak of 1953 when Hogan did those things.

Those things add up to one of the three epic years in tournament golf. To anyone who knows the difference between a wedge and a putter, Hogan's accomplishments in '53 rank right up there with what Bobby Jones did in 1930 and what Byron Nelson did in 1945.

What to call it?

La Hoganaise? Year of the Hawk?

Most generally, it is referred to as the year of Hogan's Triple Crown, but it was more than that, of course.

Hogan in '53. Hardly catchy, but that says it simply enough, and sounds as stylish as the man himself.

Hogan in '53. All caps, italics, underlined. Burned into the minds of all of us who watched him at his peak.

It was far from the end of golf, but it may have been the end of shotmaking in the artistic sense.

Let me set the stage. The deeds of Hogan in '53 came four years before Sputnik, three years before Elvis, two years before Jack Fleck, and one year before Dien Bien Phu.

In that engaging spring and summer of '53, Dwight D. Eisenhower was in his first full year as President, Joseph Stalin was buried in Russia—not a minute too soon—the Korean War was ending, the Mau Maus were uprising, and Americans were playing Scrabble when they weren't going to see *Shane* at the movies, watching *Dragnet* on TV, or singing "Till I Waltz Again with You."

I might add that I was graduating from college that year while simultaneously covering Hogan as often as possible for a Fort Worth newspaper that sometimes even paid my travel expenses.

The fire was lit for Ben in '53 by the bitter disappointments of 1952.

The year 1952, I think, was supposed to be what 1953 became. After all, Hogan had captured the Masters and the U.S. Open in 1951 and seemed to be fully recovered from the automobile accident three years earlier. And in the final round of the '51 Open at Oakland Hills, he had shot that memorable 67 on what many still consider to be the most rugged Open course in history. It remains the Rembrandt of U.S. Open final rounds.

Pardon me a minute, but I think I should explain why that round was a Rembrandt.

You see, Oakland Hills in 1951 was the kind of course where you could lose your feet in the tall, brutal rough. Yeah, Foot-Joys and all. And on those frequent occasions when the golfer would find himself on the wrong side of the green, there was usually something between his ball and the cup, either the Sahara Desert, played by a yawning, intrusive bunker, or the Himalayas, played by the fierce undulations of the putting surfaces.

Three men were responsible for the toughness of the layout. They were Joe Dey, then the executive director of the USGA, Robert Trent Jones, the architect who was brought in to "modernize" the old Donald Ross course, and John Oswald, chairman of the greens committee. It was Oswald, an engineer at the Ford Motor Company, who pushed harder than anyone for a rugged, if not impossible, course. "The Open is the greatest title there is," he said to Dey. "The course should be so hard, nobody can win it."

It almost was.

From the moment the pros saw it in their first practice round, they began to howl and complain in a way they haven't at any Open since. Cary Middlecoff said, "You have to walk down these fairways single file." Sam Snead said, "I thought I was going to a golf tournament, not on a safari." Hogan said, "If I had to play this course for a living every week, I'd get into another business."

More than one golf writer thought he had died and gone to Quote Heaven.

To fully appreciate Hogan's 67, you have to know where he came from. Sam Snead's 71 led the first day. Ben shot a 76, which left him five strokes and thirty-one players behind. "I made six mistakes," he said, "and paid for all of them." Hogan shot a 73 on Friday ("Three mistakes") as Bobby Locke, the South African, seized the lead at 144 for 36 holes. Ben was still five back.

"A couple of sixty-nines might take it tomorrow," a friend said to him that evening. "I'm afraid it's out of reach," he replied.

In those days, they played 36 the last day—"Open Saturday," as it was known. Hogan almost whipped the course in the morning round. He was three under going to the fourteenth, but he finished with a double bogey and two bogeys for a 71. He was hot, to say the least, both at himself and that course, but he was creeping up on the leaders. Locke and Jimmy Demaret were tied at 218 at noon. Hogan was at 220, now only two strokes behind.

Ben went out in 35, even par, in the afternoon, playing flawlessly, hitting "the slits." At the long tenth, he hit a driver and a "career" 2-iron to within five feet of the cup. Birdie. At the thirteenth, he birdied again with a

6-iron shot and a 14-footer. He took three from the edge for a bogey at the fourteenth. At the fifteenth, where he made a double bogey in the morning, Hogan drove with a 4-wood and then hit a 6-iron to within five feet of the hole and made it for a birdie. And he birdied the eighteenth with a driver and another 6-iron and a 15-foot putt for his 67 and winning total of 287. Clayton Heafner's 69 and 289 brought him second place. Hogan and Heafner were the only players to break 70 in the tournament, the only players to break 290. Locke finished third at 291. Poor Demaret collapsed with a 78, tied for fourteenth.

Ben Hogan shot many scores lower than 67, so why was this the greatest eighteen ever played? Well, the average score of the field that afternoon at Oakland Hills was 75. In that sense, you can say that Hogan's 67 was actually 8 under par on what he would call "the monster"—and it *was* the last round of the Open, right? Case closed.

Now to '52 and the Masters. Ben is one stroke back after 18, three back after 36, and tied with Sam Snead for the lead after 54, poised and ready on an Augusta National course that was playing windy and rougher than it had in years. This, by the way, was the "mystery Masters," as the press called it, inasmuch as Western Union was on strike that week. Writers typed, phoned in, and dictated, to the great disgust of newspaper deskmen all across the country.

What happened to Ben in that final round bruised him badly. Nothing went right, mostly around the rye greens, and he soared to a ghastly 79, finishing in a tie for seventh, as Snead won. He was embarrassed but not humiliated. As he often said, "A golfer loses a lot more tournaments than he wins."

One month later, he recovered enough to win the Colonial National Invitation in his hometown, and then went about gearing up for the U.S. Open at Northwood in Dallas.

In the first two rounds at Northwood, Hogan fired a couple of 69s and not only led by two strokes, but his total of 138 tied the existing Open record for 36 holes. Impressionable old me thought he looked uncatchable—and said as much in the Fort Worth *Press,* whose readers must have numbered dozens.

The next morning, however, before my very eyes, Ben lost that Open at Northwood's sixth hole. In today's vernacular, he "overpured" a 4-wood shot that went right at the flag but wound up behind the green, out-of-bounds by a foot. The resulting double bogey started some bleeding that didn't stop until Hogan had shot 74-74 on that long, hot Saturday. He finished third as a relatively obscure Julius Boros—obscure to me, at least—got up and down out of ten bunkers to win.

That Open was Bitter Disappointment No. 2 for the year, but all Ben said about it was: "Golf is a game of mistakes. I made too many, and maybe I let some of them bother me too much. You can't do that."

Those disappointments of '52, I am quite sure, put Hogan to work even harder for the year to come, and 1953 would be the year when he hardly made mistakes at all.

Hogan amused himself with a few pro-am appearances at the start of '53 before he got down to serious business. Mostly, he participated because of friendships or because the locales were convenient.

In January, for instance, he played in the 54-hole Thunderbird Pro-Am in Palm Springs, California, seeing as how he was spending time out there anyway, being paid to represent the Tamarisk Country Club. I might interject here that he was being paid by Tamarisk for his "name," primarily, and not to sell sweaters and golf balls.

His annual pilgrimage to Palm Beach, Florida, to Seminole, came in March. Since the automobile accident, this was where he had gone to get his game in shape for a month or longer. At Seminole, he would practice eight hours a day, hitting a bag of balls with every club in the bag, from the pitching wedge through the driver, in that order. Two or three times a week, he would have a game with friends, with the pro Claude Harmon, and Robert Sweeny, the fine amateur, and whoever also cared to summon up the nerve to join them.

Hogan played in the 36-hole Seminole Pro-Am that year, tieing for second. Shortly before the Masters, he played in one more pro-am, at 18 holes, in Aiken, South Carolina, which is just across the river from Augusta, Georgia.

Hogan then turned his attention to the Masters. With revenge somewhere in his mind, no doubt, Ben played what he would describe as "the best golf of my life" as he shot a record 274 for 72 holes, breaking the old mark by five strokes and setting a new standard that would last twelve years, until the Age of Nicklaus.

He seized the lead at 36 holes and eventually won by five shots over Porky Oliver, but it was in the third round that he took a stranglehold on the tournament with a six-under 66, a round that would rate somewhere up there near his Rembrandt in '51.

He hit every fairway and sixteen greens. The two greens he missed were only by a yard. He three-putted twice. He missed three short birdie putts. It could have been a 61 and on those hard, slick rye greens that were just as fast as today's bent but didn't hold the approach as well.

Told that he had broken the 72-hole record after winning, Ben said, "Oh? That's nice, but I was only trying to win a golf tournament."

Maybe you should understand that when Hogan competed in those days, he always commanded the largest gallery on the course. Palmer-size crowds. He would be aware of the throngs but seldom bothered by their wondrous stares.

He would touch the bill of his white cap to acknowledge their cheers and applause as he walked off a green, but he never removed the cap unless he was leaving the 72nd green assured of victory. Only then would this darkly handsome figure lavish his disciples with a broad smile.

He walked from shot to shot as quickly as he could, not so much with a limp but as if he were always trudging slightly uphill. He might study a shot for a long moment, drawing on a cigarette, peering coldly into the distance. At times, he left the impression that he was contemplating a mathematical problem so complex that perhaps only *he* could solve it. Once he selected the club, however, he played briskly. The address, the waggle, and *crack*—with that full, smooth, flat swing.

Ben was as meticulous in his dress as he was in his golf. Always a white cap. Always in conservative solid colors—tans, grays, navy blues. His attire would fit him perfectly—he had the trim build to wear clothes well.

My own notion was that if Ben Hogan had ever worn a red shirt or green slacks, he couldn't have broken 80.

After the car accident in '49, there was never any question about Ben limiting his amount of tournament play. His body simply couldn't have held up to a lengthy schedule even though he was at the top of his skills.

From 1950 on, he entered only four or five tournaments a year—in '53 it would be six. That anyone could compete so rarely and yet perform so well remains one of golf's mysteries.

Claude Harmon probably offered the best explanation once. "Only Hogan can turn it on and turn it off," said Claude.

You may ask how Hogan occupied his time the rest of the year. Well, he lived graciously in Fort Worth, he socialized some, he played the occasional exhibition round, he played country club golf with friends, he followed college football keenly, he managed his financial affairs, and he was in the oil business.

His next stop after Augusta was Mexico City in late April for the Pan American Open, primarily because he was curious to see Clube de Golfe, a highly regarded and much-talked-about course at the time. Against a fine field of Tommy Bolts and Gardner Dickinsons and Peter Thomsons, Hogan shot 286 and won the tournament by three strokes. His 68 in the third round tied for the low 18.

Four days later, he was teeing off in White Sulphur Springs, West Virginia, in the Greenbrier Pro-Am Invitational, a festival that was as much a social event as a competition. Here, Hogan shot a blazing 272 for the four rounds but it wasn't blazing enough. Snead shot 268. Ben had to settle for a tie for third place. It would be the only tournament he would lose—for shame.

And now it was back to the serious stuff. In late May came the Colonial in Fort Worth, already entrenched as a premier event on the tour—"the Masters of the Southwest." Old Colonial, back then, was one of the narrowest and most brutal courses around. This was before architect Dick Wilson, various storms, and the Corps of Engineers defanged it.

Ben won the '53 Colonial in a glide, by five strokes, with a score of 282. His finishing three-under 67 was sculpted in a high wind and gleamed as the tournament's low round.

It was Ben's fourth victory in the tournament's eight years. Thus, Colonial had become even more of a "Hogan's Alley" than the Riviera Country Club, on which he had captured a U.S. Open and two L.A. Opens.

What lay ahead for Hogan now were the U.S. Open at Oakmont in Pitttsburgh and the British Open at Carnoustie, which he had long since entered for what he knew would be the one and only time he would ever play in it.

"I'm forty years old and I've been traveling for nineteen years," he said, as if no other explanation was necessary.

It was Ben's custom to arrive a week early at an Open site to prepare himself properly. This time, he had other business to get him there early. In 1953, for some arcane reason, the USGA decided that *everybody* would have to qualify at 36 holes to get into that Open, even a man like Hogan who had won three of the past five.

Hogan didn't complain about it as much as several others, possibly because he realized he would have to kick it around Oakmont and the Pittsburgh Field Club, more or less like me, in order to miss out on one of the 150 berths. He qualified handily with casual rounds of 77 and 73. At which point he predicted that an "unknown" would win at Oakmont with a score of 292 or higher.

Joking with the press, he picked Sam Parks to win again.

Then he went out and butchered Oakmont with a five-under 67 in the opening round, and took a three-stroke lead. It would be the low round of the championship, and when you look at the 283 he shot for the 72 holes and the fact that he won by six over Snead—they were the only players to break 290—you might get the idea that it was easy for him. The fact is, it wasn't.

Snead shot a 69 to Hogan's 72 on Friday and trailed by only two. On Saturday morning, Sam's 72 to Ben's 73 left Snead only one back. The afternoon round was yet to come—and Ben would be out an hour ahead of Snead, unable to control anything but his own game.

As he grabbed a quick clubhouse lunch between eighteens on the last day, "Open Saturday," surrounded by a cluster of sportswriters, Hogan said, "This tournament could come down to the last three holes, and that's where the real danger is, particularly if you need to go for a birdie."

When Hogan arrived at the sixteenth tee on that long afternoon, he was one over for the round, needing three pars for 73 and a total of 285. He knew he was the leader but didn't know by how many, exactly, leader boards being what they were at the time. Two strokes? Possibly three? And what was a safe lead if Snead were to catch fire behind him and had several more holes to play?

Ben later said, "All you can do in a situation like that is try to play as well as you can, one hole at a time."

The shots Hogan hit over those last three holes, under the Open gun, were among the best of his career and beyond the ability of any other mortal. That's if you want the opinion of a fellow Texan.

At the lethal bunkered 234-yard par-3 sixteenth, he floated a brassie shot safely onto the center of the green and got down in two putts for what he deemed a "crucial" 3.

The old seventeenth at Oakmont was a 292-yard oddity, an uphill par 4, the green hemmed in by deep, furrowed bunkers. A sucker hole. Through three rounds, Hogan had chosen to avoid the catastrophic bunkers. He had driven short of the furrows and elected to wedge out of high grass, settling for sure pars.

This time, however, he ripped a drive. Arrow straight, it rammed through the slender entrance to the green and left him pin-high with a 30-foot putt for an eagle deuce. The putt stopped inches short. It was a tap-in birdie.

At the 462-yard eighteenth, one of the finest finishing holes in golf, Ben smacked another drive nearly 300 yards. After drawing on the ever-present cigarette, he whistled a 5-iron in there, eight feet from the cup, and sank it for yet another birdie, and a closing 71. In the heat, he had finished 3-3-3 to wrap up his fourth U.S. Open title in six years. Today, that kind of finish would be called putting your foot on their throat.

Less than two weeks later, Hogan was off for Scotland and his experience at Carnoustie. It is an often overlooked fact that Ben also had to qualify for the British Open, which he did with ease on rounds of 70 and 75, played at Burnside and Carnoustie.

Think of it. In two of three majors he won in '53, he was forced to *qualify*—to play 108 holes.

For all of his practice at Carnoustie, Hogan later related that he never got used to the slow greens or the deception of the flagsticks, some of which were seven feet high while others were only four feet high. The uneven height made judging distance a severe problem for a first-time visitor.

Although he lowered his scores in each of the four rounds, 73, 71, 70, and 68, that last one being a course record and the low round of the championship, bringing victory by four strokes, he had to labor over every short putt. He couldn't remember a single tap-in.

He trailed the fine American amateur Frank Stranahan by three shots after Wednesday's first 18. He trailed the tiny Welshman Dal Rees and Scotsman Eric Brown by two strokes at 36. After the morning 18 on Friday, he was tied for the lead with Roberto De Vicenzo at 214.

In the afternoon, he began to seize the championship, and the Triple Crown, when from out of the sand in a greenside bunker at the fifth hole he chose to chip the ball rather than explode it. He chipped it in for a birdie.

Chipping out of sand is a delicate art, of course, and you might say that a player needs to have been raised in Scotland or Texas to handle it.

When Hogan followed up that birdie with another at the "long hole," the 567-yard par-5 sixth, Ben was not so much in danger of losing the British Open as he feared being trampled by the hordes of happy Scots who all but swallowed him up on every hole.

Years later, when Hogan was asked if he had taken time to see St. Andrews on his one trip to Scotland, he replied, "No, I didn't have time. I was there for one purpose."

Ben and Valerie sailed home from Europe on a luxury liner and both were astounded at the reception. The fireboats were out squirting water when the ship entered New York Harbor. Hogan received a ticker-tape parade up Broadway, reminiscent of the one given

Bobby Jones for his Grand Slam. After three days of dinners and other celebrations in Manhattan, Ben returned to his hometown for yet another parade through the streets of downtown Fort Worth.

Hogan in '53.

He could only win five of the six tournaments he entered. He remains the only man who has won three professional majors, a Triple Crown, in the same year.

The Slam Streak Dunk?

Later that summer, I recall asking him if he had any more goals in life, other than to keep playing a while longer in the Masters, the Open, Colonial, as long as he felt competitive.

Well, yes.

He said he was thinking of designing a set of golf clubs.

The Mother of All Streaks

SOME OF MY CHUMS in the golf writing society had a merry old time one recent spring when they made a big thing out of a "streak" that Fred Couples went on, a two-month journey in which the popular fellow bagged three firsts and two seconds on the PGA Tour. Let me say that I wasn't embarrassed at the time by the flood of adjectives in which my brethren almost drowned poor Fred—I knew how starved they were for a new American hero—so I hope they weren't too disturbed by my yawns.

Not that I wasn't happy to see the boyishly handsome Couples become better known, to see his lazybones swing become more familiar to the masses, to have him endear himself to us all with his famous statement: "I never answer the phone at home—somebody may want to talk to me." That was a nice spree Couples enjoyed, a fine binge, but you wouldn't call it a "streak."

It was nothing you would carve in marble or sew on a pillow. It was hardly a performance of historic significance. It wouldn't live in infamy, or even a neighboring town, and I might add that it would die of hunger in Fort Worth, Texas, where Byron Nelson and Ben Hogan come from, not to forget me, your dogged statistician.

As an old streak watcher, I know a streak when I see one. A streak is when the Oklahoma Sooners win 47 football games in a row. A streak is when Joe DiMaggio hits safely in 56 straight games. A streak is when Joe Louis passes through my entire childhood knocking out Bums of the Month. Real streaks don't eat quiche.

In golf, I also know that streaks were defined once and for all by Byron Nelson.

Most grown-ups of the golf persuasion are aware of the grandest streak in the history of the game. I speak of 1945, when Byron won 11 tournaments in a row and 18 for the year. What most grown-ups of the golf persuasion do not realize, however, is that Nelson's streak started in 1944 and ran through much of 1946.

Before I get to that, I think I should point out that Byron is probably the nicest, warmest, friendliest immortal that ever came down a fairway. As a kid, I was lucky to see him in his prime. We became friendly later and enjoyed a lot of discussions, at my prodding, about how it was back then.

Golf's grandest streak couldn't have happened to a better person. Now then.

Not a lot has ever been said about 1944 because it gets confused with 1943, which was the dreariest and most inactive year in the annals of American sport. World War II brought an end to everything in '43 except for

Notre Dame football and Stan Musial's bat with the St. Louis Cardinals.

But things began to look up in '44. Italy had surrendered—it was one down and two to go where the war was concerned. So the PGA Tour made a comeback with 22 tournaments. That was when a tall, fast-playing Texan began to be known to newspaper poets as "Lord Byron Nelson, golf's mechanical man."

Nelson won eight of those 22 events, four in a row at one point, and was either first, second, or third in 17 out of the 22. His worst finish in '44 was a tie for sixth at Oakland. Horrors.

Suddenly, he was a familiar figure in sport, a *presence.* As Bobby Jones had become familiar in his knickers and necktie, Nelson was an idol in a white visor, white golf shirt, brown slacks, brown shoes, a shotmaker deluxe with a gloveless grip, upright swing, a straight hitter, a fire-at-the-pin type of player.

Incredibly, he was not a great putter. He used an old blade putter, one with loft.

"You needed some loft on the putter in those days," he would remark later. "Some of the greens we putted on weren't in the best of condition." To put it mildly.

Anyhow, then came 1945. Nelson started off by finishing either first or second in the first eight tournaments, three of which were won by Sam Snead. The illustrious streak began on March 11 when Byron teamed up with Jug McSpaden to win the Miami Four-Ball. Next came a tough victory in the Charlotte Open, where he had to go 36 holes to beat Snead in a playoff. After that, it was magic time. Nelson won the Greensboro Open by eight strokes, the Durham Open by five, the Atlanta Open by nine, the Montreal Open by ten, the Philadelphia Invitational by two, the Chicago Victory Open by seven, the PGA Championship in Dayton, Ohio, at match play where he defeated Gene Sarazen, Mike Turnesa, Denny Shute, Claude Harmon, and Sam Byrd in that order, the Tam O'Shanter back in Chicago by eleven, and the Canadian Open by four.

The streak didn't end until August 19, when he wound up in a tie for fourth at Memphis. Thus, Nelson went five months—*five months,* pardon my shouting—without losing a golf tournament.

It's a footnote to the streak that Byron came back the week after Memphis to win the Knoxville Invitational by ten strokes in a field that included, among others, Ben Hogan and Sam Snead. In those days, the others often included Jimmy Demaret, Craig Wood, Henry Picard, Vic Ghezzi, Dick Metz, Jug McSpaden, Johnny Revolta, Porky Oliver, Dutch Harrison, Lloyd Mangrum, Lawson Little, Ralph Guldahl, Toney Penna, Ky Laffoon, Clayton Heafner, George Fazio, Herman Barron, and Frank Stranahan. Which is to say that Byron wasn't exactly whipping up on dog meat.

And what of 1946? Well, after all of the aforementioned, Nelson started off in '46 by winning the first two tournaments of the year, the L.A. Open at Riviera by five and the San Francisco Open at Olympic by nine. Considering that he had captured the last two events he entered in '45, the Seattle Open by a mere thirteen shots and the Glen Garden Invitational in Fort Worth by eight, this gave him four in a row again, or one of those minor streaks that's been overlooked.

He then took some time off and began to think seriously about retirement. The constant pressure of trying to live up to everyone's expectations was burning a hole in what had always been a weak and unruly stomach anyhow. He went ahead and competed sporadically through the rest of '46, entering twenty-one tournaments in all. Guess what. He won six of them and even tied for the U.S. Open at Canterbury in Cleveland but lost by a slim one stroke to Lloyd Mangrum in what became a grueling 36-hole playoff.

He *did* retire at the end of '46, at the astonishingly tender age of thirty-four. Among the game's immortals, only Bobby Jones, at twenty-eight, quit competitive golf at a younger age than Nelson.

The arithmetic for this amazing three-year period shows that Byron won 32 of the 72 tournaments he entered. That's very nearly half of them, folks. The arithmetic also shows that he was either first, second, or third in 57 out of the 72.

If I were an exclamation point user, there wouldn't be any left by now. In today's world, he would have earned a different nickname—Lord Barbarian Nelson, golf's Terminator Predator.

Through all of this mischief, Nelson's lone finish *out* of the top 10 was a tie for thirteenth place at Pensacola one February week of 1946, which prompted the wisecracking Jimmy Demaret to observe, "I've been telling you all along he's overrated."

Old Tom

AT A GOLF TOURNAMENT many years ago, I was inspired to make the brilliant joke in a Texas newspaper that if Tommy Bolt had not become a touring pro, he would in all probability have been married to Bonnie Parker. The following day when I saw Bolt at the Colonial Country Club in Fort Worth, he asked me who Bonnie Parker was. I guess I got about two sentences deep into the history of Clyde Barrow and Bonnie Parker—ever grinning, politely, ever alert for the orbiting wedge—when Bolt said, "Well, son, why don't you just go out and round up them two and Old Tom will play their low ball."

As a journalist, I loved Tommy Bolt. Talk about good copy. But Tommy Bolt the golfer, the stylish shotmaker, was an artist I was often tempted to put up there with Ben Hogan. Those of us who saw him perform in his prime recognized that when Thomas Henry Bolt was right—confident, calm, all tempo, and not blaming Arnold Palmer or the Lord for any short putts that curled out of the cup—no other human being could strike a prettier variety of shots, or land them more softly on the greens, other than Hogan, of course.

On the subject of Hogan, whom Tommy always credited with "weakening" his grip, curing his terminal hook, Bolt once said, "Now lookie here at all these baby-face mullets on the tour. They come out here dressed up in their Ben Hogan blues and grays. They ought to come to Old Tom and let him show 'em how to match their reds with their pinks and their fuchsias."

It was at Southern Hills in Tulsa where Bolt strung together some of his, and history's, finest golf. This was in the 1958 U.S. Open, the first major to be held at Southern Hills, and Southern Hills was determined to make an impression on the field.

The course presented an arrangement of fairways as narrow as Bolt's 4-wood and a Bermuda rough that was not only calf-deep but as gnarled as Tommy's temper could be. But he finessed the layout, led all the way, and won laughing, by four strokes.

I must tell you how good that was. Of the game's other big stars of the era, only Julius Boros and Gene Littler were heard from at Southern Hills, and they finished six and seven shots behind Bolt. Sam Snead missed the cut. Jimmy Demaret withdrew. Cary Middlecoff was seventeen strokes back, and Ben Hogan, his wrist slightly sprained in a bout with the rough, wound up in a tie for tenth.

The most dangerous hole at Southern Hills is the twelfth, a par 4 requiring a straight drive and a cautious iron shot or else you have to deal with rough, trees, and water. Bolt birdied the twelfth the first three rounds and parred it on the last eighteen. He was three under on the hole that took everyone else virtually out of contention.

This was the Open that furnished Tommy Bolt Story No. 1,032. When Tommy entered the press tent after 36 holes as the sole owner of the lead, he pretended to be angry at a Tulsa writer. There had been a misprint in the morning paper. Old Tom was forty years old at the time, but the paper had said he was forty-nine. The Tulsa writer apologized for the typographical error.

"Typographical error, hell," Bolt said. "It was a perfect four and a perfect nine."

None of us who were privileged to be near him, inside the ropes—it was still permitted then—would be likely to forget some of the dialogue that took place over the last few holes as Old Tom closed in on his victory at Southern Hills.

Three of us actually walked along in the middle of the fairways with him. With me were Bud Shrake, a newspaper cohort and old friend, and Jimmy Breslin, who was then with the NEA feature service in New York. This was before Shrake and Breslin had become successful book authors.

"Ain't this something?" Bolt said, mostly to me. "Old Tom's gonna win hisself a Ben Hogan type of tournament. How 'bout that, pard?"

Going up the eighteenth fairway now, the last hole of the championship, after Bolt had put a glorious 4-wood on the green, Breslin said to him, "You're going to win it, you ought to throw a club."

Bolt mumbled something about a book he had been reading, a book that had given him "inner peace," he said.

"Inner peace don't sell newspapers," Breslin said. "You don't throw a club, how come you got the name?"

Tommy replied, "If I threw as many clubs as everybody says, the manufacturers wouldn't have nothin' to do but manufacture Tommy Bolt golf clubs."

"You could throw a little one," Breslin said. "Something you don't need."

Bolt looked at Shrake and me, as if to ask how Jimmy Breslin ever got admitted to a golf tournament.

Jimmy dropped back a few paces and said, more or less to himself, "The story don't work."

Old Tom's reputation as terrible-tempered, tempestuous Tommy (Thunder) Bolt was enhanced by the wire services, of course, just as they made Hogan a lifetime bantamweight, kept Cary Middlecoff a Dr., and insisted Byron Nelson was both a British lord and a mechanical man.

What Bolt did best as a shotmaker was turn the tee shot in any direction he wanted—he could play the doglegs like a violin—strike better fairway woods than anybody, and flirt with the flagsticks on his short irons.

He seemed to make the ball land more softly than anyone else, and there was no explaining it, except that his feeling for the shots must have had something to do with it. As he often said, "Son, I can poop one into the water and it don't even splash."

That Bolt did not win more than fifteen tournaments during his ten good years on the PGA Tour was probably a result of timing, as in career timing. His early good years were also some of Hogan's and Snead's best, and then later on his career bumped into the rise of Arnold Palmer.

Perhaps Old Tom knew he was never destiny's child, and maybe this is why, now and then, after blowing a short putt, he would look up at the sky, and say, "Why don't You come on down here and play me *one* time?"

Not that a few putts here and there would not have

improved the record of the man who came out of Ha-
worth, Oklahoma, moved through Louisiana, and settled in Texas to learn the game. He was close in a few
other U.S. Opens as well as the Masters twice, and a couple of times he reached the semifinals of the PGA when
that major was conducted at match play, knocking off
such players as Sam Snead (twice), Gene Littler, and Lew
Worsham, but then he would get knocked off by a
Claude Harmon, a Jackson Bradley, or a Charles
Prentice.

All of which prompted Old Tom to say at one point,
"Who wants to win a tournament that don't have nobody in it but a bunch of mother geese?"

Tommy Bolt Story No. 4,345:

At a time when Ed Sneed, an accomplished tour
player later on, was still an amateur he found himself
paired with Bolt in a Cincinnati pro-am one day. Sneed
admired Bolt greatly and wanted to play well enough to
impress the legendary shotmaker. They came to a par-3
hole that required an 8-iron but you had to be cautious
of water behind the green. Ed Sneed hit a high, wild
right-to-left shot that flew to the back of the green and
bounced into the water.

Bolt then teed up his own ball and said casually, "Old
Ed knows what makes the ball go. Those hooks really
go, don't they, son?"

Tommy Bolt Story No. 5,689:

One day Bolt was trying to line up a putt during a
round at a tour event—it doesn't matter where—and
slowly he backed away, looking irritated. From the gallery behind him, it seems, a spectator's shadow had in-
advertently obscured Tommy's view. Characteristically,
Tommy's chin jutted out, and he said to no one in particular, "Well, I never could read *Poa annua* in the dark!"

When terrible-tempered, tempestuous Tommy (Thunder) Bolt won that U.S. Open back in 1958, a fellow named Tom Watson was only eight years old, Ben Crenshaw was only six years old, and people like Fred Couples and Paul Azinger hadn't even been born. Thus, it was both startling and sad for me to realize that whole generations of golfers on the American tour had missed Tommy Bolt.

This, I suppose, was for them.

The Towering Inferno

ON THE GOLF COURSE at the peak of his game, Tom Weiskopf was one part Jack Nicklaus, one part Tommy Bolt, and, for better or worse, one part Tom Weiskopf, which was something of a problem. Off the golf course, he was always completely Tom Weiskopf, which was sometimes another problem. Well, look. It wasn't easy being the first next-Nicklaus.

Weiskopf became the first next-Nicklaus in the late 1960s, soon after everyone recognized what a beautiful swing he had—the graceful arc encircling a perfect grip—what dazzling length he had, and what finesse around the greens he had. All this to go along with his power and natural ability, as undisciplined as it was.

Tom was ordained the first next-Nicklaus ahead of such other next-Nicklauses as Johnny Miller, Ben Crenshaw, Tom Watson, and Greg Norman. Of course, none of them ever had a chance to actually be the next

Nicklaus because, among other things, God wouldn't allow it.

However, where raw talent was concerned, Weiskopf probably had the best chance to become something close to Nicklaus. This is not to say that he squandered the opportunity, although by never missing a social occasion, and never truly wanting to carry the heavy burden of being a living, practicing immortal, he may have squandered some of it, but I, of course, would be the last writer in the press tent to blame a person for choosing life over golf.

It was frequently said that Tom's mind got in the way of his golf. This was a knock that many observers put on him, largely those who didn't take the trouble to get to know him better. It was often written that there was nothing standing between Tom Weiskopf and greatness that a brain transplant couldn't cure.

I don't think this bothered Tom much, for he knew the same thing had been said of Sam Snead.

You had to understand that when Weiskopf was rude or thoughtless or short-tempered with other competitors or fans or writers, he was only mad at himself—well, maybe the greenkeeper, too, at times—but this mood never lasted very long. He could easily be defused by a joke, or the prospect of a beverage and good conversation with good company, or the potential of a night on the town.

Much like his early idol, Tommy Bolt, he expected a golf shot struck with style and perfection to be rewarded with a perfect result. When it wasn't, Weiskopf could turn into the Towering Inferno, just as Bolt was known to become Thunder Bolt and tempestuous Tommy at the sight of a bad bounce.

Bolt had an influence on Weiskopf's attire. Well-

tailored, vivid colors marked Weiskopf's appearance—
flaming red, bright blue funk, birdie green. "You know
what Bolt always said," Weiskopf liked to remark. "If
you lose your crease, you get to walk in."

Call Weiskopf immature in those days, as some did,
and he would respond that he was merely "colorful," as
Bolt had been colorful—temper and all. "Sports need
more color," Weiskopf would say to a friend. "Don't
you think?"

There was this afternoon at Royal Lytham during the
1979 British Open when Tom and I dropped in on one
of those hospitality tents. Across the room, he quickly
spotted Ilie Nastase, the temperamental tennis star.

"There's a guy I think is colorful," Tom said. "I like
Nastase, I don't care what they say about him. He gets a
bad rap—like me—but we need more color in sports."

Weiskopf invited himself to join Nastase's table,
whereupon Tom began to tell Nastase how much he enjoyed and approved of Nastase's temper tantrums on
the tennis courts.

"You're colorful," Tom said. "*I'm* colorful—what's
wrong with that?"

Nastase only stared at him, as if to say, "Who *are* you?"

One evening at dinner that week in the elegant Clif-
ton Arms, where Weiskopf was in the company of
myself and our mutual good friend Ed Sneed, Tom decided we should have the finest wine in that part of England.

He summoned the maître d', whose name was Dieter,
and commanded Dieter to bring us a bottle of something ancient, red, dusty, and expensive.

The wine was brought. Tom sipped it and made a
face.

"This is terrible," Tom said to Dieter. "Bring me a bucket of ice and some club soda."

Ed Sneed and I exchanged fearful glances.

Moments later, Weiskopf filled a water glass half full with the expensive grape, dumped in a handful of ice cubes, loaded up the rest of the glass with club soda. He then took a swig, looked pleased and seriously announced, "Now *this* is a good glass of wine."

Ed Sneed didn't fall on the carpet in laughter, but he came close.

I have always liked to claim a tiny shred of credit for helping Weiskopf win his only major, the 1973 British Open at Troon.

The truth is, he hated the place before the championship began—the course, his hotel, the food, the weather, and every clump of shrubbery in Scotland.

On the morning of the first round, I ran into him and listened to his list of woes.

"You can have this place," he said. "Being here is like camping out. The golf course is a zoo. What do you think of the bacon and eggs, huh? How about your *bathroom*?" He went on about the bewildering atrocities of Troon's layout.

Finally, I said, "Hogan never liked a golf course very much at a major. Ben thought the course was his enemy. He went out and tried to kill it."

Tom dwelled on this news for a moment. You could almost see the cartoonist's lightbulb being drawn above his head.

"That's what I'll do!" he said. "I'll go out and kill it."

Which is what he did, in the most spectacular golf of his career. His 72-hole total of 276 in that gray, misty, breezy tournament over the narrow stretches and sometimes hidden targets of Troon tied the British Open record at the time.

Those who saw it would never forget that third round when Weiskopf and Johnny Miller were paired together, fighting for control of the championship. Miller was fresh from winning the U.S. Open at Oakmont and near the peak of his own game. They waged an astounding duel, one on one, but Tom got the best of it. If Miller hit it close, Weiskopf hit it closer. If Miller hit it stiff, Weiskopf hit it stiffer.

After that championship, Weiskopf decided he loved England and Scotland, loved the British Open. Ever since then, his personalized license plate has said "T-R-O-O-N."

As Tom tells it on himself, his finest single round of golf was back in America, in Jacksonville, Florida, in that time during the 1970s before the Players Championship replaced the Greater Jacksonville Open on the tour.

It was a week when he found himself out of contention, and he was confronted with an early-morning tee time that was far too early for a person who had been held hostage at an all-night piano concert.

He remembers Ed Sneed driving him to the course at Nigel Mansell speed. He hopped, stepped, and jumped to the first tee, struggling to put on his cleats along the way. He thought to himself: Walter Hagen never had it this tough.

He bogeyed the first two holes, then drove into the rough at the third. This was where he asked for the greatest ruling in the history of golf.

Presently, the late Clyde Mangum, then rules chief of the PGA Tour, arrived in a golf cart. He found Tom leaning against a tree trunk.

"What's the problem, Tom?" Clyde asked. "Looks like you've got a pretty good lie."

Weakly, Weiskopf said, "Clyde, can you get me an egg sandwich and a carton of milk?"

Mangum did, and Weiskopf shot six under par from there in.

To this day, Weiskopf thinks it may be the best round of golf a dead man ever played.

Throughout all of his first next-Nicklaus years, I always thought Tom embodied that lyric from "The Pilgrim: Chapter 33," one of Kris Kristofferson's best songs, the lyric that goes: "*He's a walking contradiction, partly truth and partly fiction, taking every wrong direction on his lonely way back home.*"

Tom was certainly an original, and for this reason I wasn't surprised to see him become an expert golf commentator on TV as well as a very good course architect. As much as for his wonderful shotmaking ability, Tom may be remembered for a comment he made on the air during CBS's Masters telecast of 1986, when Nicklaus was winning his sixth green coat. As Jack stood on the sixteenth tee in the final round, performing what amounted to a miracle, here was Weiskopf, a four-time Masters runner-up, being asked what Nicklaus was thinking about in that crucial moment.

Quickly, Weiskopf said on the air, "If I knew what was going through Jack Nicklaus's head, I would have won this golf tournament."

Now *that* was colorful, Tom.

The Masters
Its Ownself

SOMETHING MYSTICAL happens to every writer who goes to the Masters for the first time, some sort of emotional experience that results in a search party having to be sent out to recover his typewriter from a clump of azaleas. The writer first becomes hypnotized by the "cathedral of pines," down around the tenth fairway normally; then he genuflects at the Sarazen Bridge on the fifteenth, and eventually takes up a position on the Augusta National veranda, there to wait for an aging wisteria vine to crawl up his sleeve and caress his priceless clubhouse badge. It is a peculiar state of mind, a sort of sporting heaven in which the writer feels that if Bobby Jones could only waggle a hickory shaft once more, it would instantly turn him into F. Scott Damon "Ring" Hemingway. My own problem is that I still feel this way after more than forty consecutive years of covering this unique event.

Where has the time gone? Yesterday it was 1951. I'm a college sophomore but a working journalist following Ben Hogan every step of the way to report on the color of Ben's slacks and the contents of Valerie's thermos to the readers of the now-deceased Fort Worth *Press*. Now it's all these years later but I'm still a fixture in my favorite area, the upstairs grill and balcony, wondering how much fun it would have been to have stood around there with Granny Rice and Bob Jones.

As it is, I make do with an assortment of rogues: golfers, ex-pro football players, TV folks, poets, and other privileged souls who turn up in the clubhouse every year. I'm accused of having done a record amount of time in the upstairs grill and on that balcony overlooking the veranda. It's true that I've spent a lot of hours up there, but I can tell you that eggs, country ham, biscuits, red-eye gravy, a pot of coffee, a morning paper, a table by the window, and the idle chitchat of competitors, authors, and philosophers hasn't exactly been a bad way to start off each day at the Masters all these years.

That room, the upstairs Men's Grill, was once the interview area, so designated by those writers who wished to include quotes in their stories. Strangely enough, not every writer wanted quotes in his story forty years ago. Many believed that their own observations were all their readers deserved. I was always a quote guy, trained by Blackie Sherrod, my mentor, a Texas sportswriting legend, to pick up the good quote, not just any old quote. So trained were a few other writers, such as my old friend Bob Drum, then with the Pittsburgh *Press*.

In those early 1950s, we would ordinarily have the daily leaders all to ourselves upstairs at the completion of their rounds. Then more quote guys began coming out of the dogwood as the press corps of the Masters started to double, triple, and upward. And suddenly one year, Hogan and Snead found themselves being smothered on separate sofas while journalists stood, knelt, and shouted, "What'd you hit to the sixth?" . . . "How long was the putt on twelve?" . . . "Where was the pin on fifteen?" They practically swung from chandeliers.

This was the first time I heard Ben use a line he would rely on again in the future. He said, "One of these days a deaf-mute is going to win a golf tournament, and you guys won't be able to write a story."

Cliff Roberts, the Masters chairman, observed this scene one day, saw things were getting out of hand, and ordered an interview room installed in the press building, which used to be a tent and then a Quonset hut before it became a structure to accommodate the largest number of journalists who attend any of the four majors. The problem these days with the interview area is that the interviews themselves have become so orchestrated by Masters edict that the interview area is quite possibly the worst place in Augusta, Georgia, to look for news. Locker rooms and grill rooms are still the best places to find out things you don't know—at the Masters or any other golf tournament.

Thinking back on all of the Masters Tournaments to which I've been assigned, I'm sure that my affection for the event has something to do with the fact that such folklore characters as Ben Hogan, Sam Snead, Arnold Palmer, Jack Nicklaus, Gary Player, Ray Flord, Tom Watson, Seve Ballesteros, Ben Crenshaw, and Nick Faldo had the wisdom and moral fiber to win most of them for me.

It's only human (some sportswriters are human) and

even built into the craft that the words come easier, more quickly, and often more engagingly if the winner is already accepted by the world as a certified immortal or celebrity. Names make news, to be sure, and names have absolutely made the Masters. It wasn't Gene Kunes who holed out that shot for a double eagle, it was Gene Sarazen. And if there's anybody who likes a name more than a sportswriter, it's his boss. This is the guy back in the office who can be relied upon to create more space for your gifted prose and fatten the headline if the Masters winner is a familiar personality. I once worked for a managing editor at *Sports Illustrated* who was a great man in most ways, except that he tended to hold me personally responsible when Palmer or Nicklaus failed to win the Masters—or any other major, for that matter. I'm determined that the closest I ever came to being sentenced to a penal colony was back in 1971 at Augusta when I committed the heinous crime of Charles Coody, and again in 1973 when I was guilty of Tommy Aaron.

There is, of course, something else that helps shape the Masters into this very special event, a week to which many of us have become so devoted we can't even tolerate the thought of not being there. It's the set decoration, which is another way of saying it's the atmosphere.

The atmosphere surrounds you in two ways at the Augusta National. First of all, there's the ever-present awareness of the beauty of the course—its hills, valleys, forests, ponds, flower beds—even when you aren't especially looking at any of it. And then there are all of the old friends and associates with whom you congregate each spring over a five- or six-day period for no other purpose than to eat, drink, watch, and listen to golf.

Listening to golf becomes as important as anything if you're a writer. Much of it involves listening to the tales one hears in the locker rooms, bars, grillrooms, and dining rooms, although you generally can't print most of these tales without causing wholesale divorces. But there's also outdoor listening, to the roars from out on the course. You learn to interpret the roars.

Let's say, for example, that it's one o'clock in the afternoon, that you know Nicklaus teed off at 12:24, and you hear a roar from down in the valley. That qualifies the seasoned vet to turn immediately to someone on the veranda and calmly say, "Jack birdied two."

Most often, you'll be right. Minutes later the fact will be substantiated when a number goes up on the gigantic leader board that confronts the veranda from an age-old spot between the eighteenth and tenth fairways.

Learning to interpret roars over the years allows you to make other observations, such as:

"Watson eagled thirteen."

"How could Seve birdie ten after that drive?"

"Arnold must have hitched up his pants."

It seems to me that the old roars were more revealing, if not more fun. The loudest and most passionate roars were always those for Palmer, whereas the longest and most approving were always for Hogan. Sam Snead's roars, as I recall, never equaled Hogan's, just as the roars for Nicklaus when he was at his best never quite matched Arnold's when he was at *his* best.

Today's roars have a boring kind of sameness to them, I think. This could be a statement about the current demographics of the Masters galleries. While the crowds are still mannerly—a guy doesn't want to lose his badge, after all—they may not be as knowledgeable as they once were. I don't miss the old roars as much as I simply distrust the roars of the '90s. I mean, it could be Craig

Parry, Vijay Singh, Brett Ogle—almost anybody—who
made that eagle these days.

I probably remember the 1954 Masters more vividly
than any of the others. No doubt it has something to do
with the fact that Hogan and Snead were involved, and
it was only my fourth year there, and I was still as awed
as a teenager standing around a country club swimming
pool decorated with shapely adorables.

I'm not willing to argue that the '54 Masters was the
most thrilling of them all. The competition is too stiff.
There was 1960, for example, the tournament where
Arnold Palmer roared out of nowhere to introduce Ken
Venturi to serious heartbreak. Venturi was in the clubhouse, looking like a sure winner, when Arnold birdied
the last two holes to beat him. This was the start of something—something called Arnold Palmer.

There was 1962 when Palmer birdied two of the last
three holes to tie Gary Player and Dow Finsterwald, and
then dusted them off in an 18-hole playoff during
which the scoreboard operators showed no favoritism
whatsoever when they posted "GO ARNIE" signs all over
the golf course. And I couldn't overlook 1975, the year a
trim, now-beloved Jack Nicklaus waged a Sunday birdie
war—and won—over Tom Weiskopf and Johnny Miller.

But 1954 was special. It was important, too, because
Hogan and Snead, the two great players of the era, were
in it all the way and wound up in a tie that forced a
playoff. And the tournament proper was all the more
exciting because of Billy Joe Patton, an obscure amateur
from North Carolina. He very nearly won, and would
have if he'd known how to play safe at the thirteenth and
fifteenth holes in the final round.

The last round began with Hogan in the lead by three
strokes over Snead. Keep in mind that this was a Ben

Hogan who had merely scored a Triple Crown the year before by capturing the Masters, the U.S. Open, and the British Open, and this was a Sam Snead who had merely won the Masters twice and the PGA twice in the four previous years. We're talking legends here.

Meanwhile, there was Billy Joe Patton, who had never won anything. Which I largely attributed to his fast backswing. Nevertheless, Billy Joe had stolen the hearts of the huge crowds, not to forget the press, by taking every conceivable risk on the course and babbling about it with everybody in the gallery. Billy Joe had surprisingly led through 18 and 36, but now he trailed by five—only not for long that Sunday.

My friend Bob Drum and I, being quote guys, went out early with Billy Joe. Ben and Sam—and the tournament—would come along later. At the sixth hole, a par 3 that then had an enormous hump in the green (a mound that was once known as "the hill where they buried the elephant"), it will be to my everlasting embarrassment that I left Drum in the crowd behind the green and went to a nearby concession stand only seconds before Billy Joe struck his tee shot. The roar was deafening, similar to the kind we would hear for Palmer in later years, only this one trailed off in irregular Rebel whoops. Billy Joe had made a hole in one.

"What did it look like?" I said, having rushed back to Drum.

"It looked like a hole in one, whaddaya think it looked like?"

Drum, a large man who was even larger then, has a guttural Irish voice that has often been compared with the percussion section of the Ohio State band.

"Did it go in on the fly, bounce in, roll in, or what?" I wondered.

"It looked like a one!" said Drum, a man not known for his patience, a writer who cared little for detail in those days. "Here's the cup and here's the ball. The ball did this. That's a one!"

He scribbled something on a pairing sheet.

"Here, this is what a two looks like," he said. "That's not as good as a one. Okay? Let's go before Mush Mouth's gallery tramples us."

Mush Mouth was every golfer or writer Drum ever knew who came from the Old South.

I suppose I should interject that Drum and I became friends in the first place when we had been accidentally seated next to each other in the press emporium at my first Masters. Who could resist striking up a friendship with a man who would lean back and laugh so raucously, so often, at his own copy? I confess that he would catch me doing the same thing on occasion. We were to joke in future years that if Arnold Palmer had ever actually said the things we made up for him, he could have had his own lounge act in Vegas.

But back to '54 and Billy Joe. The amateur reclaimed the Masters lead that Sunday after he birdied the eighth and ninth holes, and by the time he reached the par-5 thirteenth, the Masters was his to win or lose.

We were standing within a few feet of Billy Joe at the thirteenth after his drive had come to rest in an awkward lie in the upper right-hand rough. He pulled a spoon out of the bag, and Drum and I looked at each other. A wooden club from a bad lie in the rough to a green guarded by water? When you're leading the Masters? On Sunday? When maybe you can be the last amateur ever to win a major? When you've probably got Hogan and Snead beaten—and we've got Pulitzers riding on it?

Billy Joe only grinned at us and the crowd, and said, "I didn't get where I am by playin' safe!"

"Great!" Drum said to me. "Where does this guy want his body shipped?"

Billy Joe didn't hear my pal, not that it would have mattered. All week long, Billy Joe had heard nothing but his own muse. And he was too far away to hear his shot when it splashed in the creek. He made a seven. Minutes later, at the fifteenth he did it again—went for the green on his second. He found the water again, made a six. History books record that Billy Joe Patton played those two holes in three over par that Sunday, holes he could easily have parred by laying up, and he only missed tying Hogan and Snead by one stroke. With those pars, he would have won the Masters by two.

Even touring pros are sometimes aware of historic importance. Many in the field stayed over on Monday to watch the Hogan-Snead playoff. Bob Jones and Cliff Roberts rode along in a golf cart. From tee to green, it was a clinic, but neither player could make a putt on those old scratchy but lightning rye greens. They used to say you could actually hear the ball rolling across the barren rye. Snead won with a two-under 70 to Hogan's 71, and the difference was a 30-foot chip shot that Sam holed from just off the tenth green.

I lost a hundred dollars to Drum on the playoff, a hundred dollars that neither of us had. Knowing he admired Hogan's game as much as I did, I later asked him why he had wanted to bet on Snead.

"It ain't the Open," he had said, having outsmarted me again.

While it's true that I missed seeing Billy Joe's ace, I wasn't always in the wrong place at Augusta. On the night before Art Wall, Jr., birdied five of the last six holes to win the 1959 Masters, I ran into him in the lobby of the ancient Bon Air Hotel, once the only place to stay before it became a retirement home. The Bon Air was headquarters for everyone, just as the old Town Tavern in downtown Augusta used to be the only place to stand in line and try to bribe your way in for dinner.

Art and I were making small talk that evening when he was recognized by one of your typical Augusta fans, a red-faced, overbeveraged Southerner in an ill-fitting blazer.

"Hey!" the man said. "Ain't you Art Wall?"

Art smiled, nodded.

"Ain't you the fellow who's supposed to make all them hole in ones?"

"That's him," I said.

"Thirty or forty of them suckers? Something like that?"

"It's up to thirty-four now," said Art politely.

"*Thirty-four?*" the man frowned. "Boy, who you tryin' to kid? Bobby didn't make but *three!*"

At a more recent Masters, I was lolling around on the veranda with Mike Lupica, a columnist for the New York *Daily News*. He's considerably younger than I—this was maybe his second Masters—and I guess I momentarily forgot that Mike is noted for his mouth. He was thumbing through the Green Book, the press guide, looking for lore items, when he said, "Your first year was fifty-one?"

"Yeah."

He started to count something.

Then he said, "Do you realize your first year was only the fifteenth Masters they'd played?"

I'd never thought of it that way.

"I'll be damned," I muttered, feeling some strange

sense of accomplishment at having seen so many of them, of having outlasted so many old friends.

"So what about it, old-timer?" he said with a glint. "Were the greens really *that* fast in those days?"

I almost made the mistake of answering him seriously. Happily, a wisteria vine grabbed me around the neck and prevented it.

Back to Baltus Oak

THE OPEN CHAMPIONSHIP of the United States Golf Association—our National Open—is a tournament with its own flavor, personality, look, attitude, atmosphere, continuity, history, mystique, and charm. It is surely the most important championship a golfer can win, which is why it is more often lost than won. As Cary Middlecoff once said—to me, actually—"Nobody wins the Open, it wins you."

If you've never been to a National Open, or never followed one very closely, you may be curious as to what it is like. Well, it is sort of like . . .

OPEN FIELD MAY REVOLT

OYSTER BISQUE, N.Y. — A glittering field on the eve of the National Open golf championship agreed today that there is so much exotic plant life bordering the narrow fairways of historic old Baltus Oak Country Club that only a skinny fashion model wearing leotards could walk down the middle of them without snagging a garment.

During today's final warm-up round, two foursomes

actually got lost in the waist-high rough on the back nine and had to be rescued by helicopters.

Curtis Strange, a former Open champion and one of those rescued, said, "If I'd wanted to hunt animals, I'd have gone to Africa!"

Deane Beman, commissioner of the PGA Tour, said he was encouraging as many touring pros as he could to withdraw from the championship.

Beman said, "As talented as our players are, they should not be subjected to this kind of embarrassment."

M. Traxton Hudspeth, president of the USGA, defended Baltus Oak, saying it belonged in the same category with Oakland Hills, Oakmont, Oak Hill, Oak Tree, and Olympic, "which sounds like oak, when you think about it."

UNKNOWN LEADS OPEN

OYSTER BISQUE, N.Y. — Jesse Ray Rives, an unheralded driving range pro from Hoot, Utah, grabbed the opening round lead in the National Open here today with a sizzling even-par 70 on historic old Baltus Oak, the course where Bobby Jones first wore knickers.

Rives, who wore coveralls and a straw hat with a band on it that said "Martha's Truck Stop," birdied the first nine holes and blew out all of the computers in the press tent. Although he came back in 44, his score held up against an array of glamorous challengers.

Incredibly, Rives took only six putts for the round, tying a record set by Bob Rosburg. He tied another record held by Gary Player when he holed out eight sand wedges.

Rives, twenty-five, said he would feel better about his chances if he weren't so lonely so far away from home.

"I wisht my uncle Clyde and my pet bobcat was here," he said.

OPEN JOLTED BY SECOND MYSTERY MAN

OYSTER BISQUE, N.Y. — R. J. "Bo" Mackey, an obscure pro at a putt-putt course in Clump, California, seized the halfway lead in the National Open here tonight when he added a 65 to his first-round 81 for a 36-hole total of 146, only six over par on historic old Baltus Oak, the course where Walter Hagen suffered his first hangover.

Having teed off at 5:14 A.M., Mackey was one of the day's early finishers at four o'clock in the afternoon as the field of 150 moved along briskly despite the 101-degree heat. Sweating out his lead in Baltus Oak's non-air-conditioned clubhouse, Mackey had some anxious moments until shortly before midnight when defending champion Jack Nicklaus finished.

Nicklaus had threatened to overtake Mackey until the seventeenth hole. Jack finished with a horrendous 13 and then a 15 on the last green when several real estate developers seemed to be clawing at him on his backswing.

Nicklaus failed to make the 36-hole cut, but did not act disappointed.

"The fact is, I'm tired of golf," said Jack. "All I really want to do is design courses now, provided there's ample beachfront property."

First-round leader Jesse Rives also failed to make the cut, largely because a lurking animal—believed by some to be a bobcat—swallowed his ball on the tenth fairway.

Mackey, who wore khakis and a tool dresser's helmet, confessed that he had received a lot of help in molding his game. He said he owed a lot to the crew on the B. W. Roberts No. 2 oil rig in Clump. They had encouraged him to leave town, he said. He also specifically singled out two men who had pieced together his compact swing: Ralph Tibitt, his ex-warden, and Roy Sangry, his parole officer.

UNKNOWN LOG JAM IN OPEN

OYSTER BISQUE, N.Y. — Billy Tom Riddle, an assistant pro from Whiskey Valley, Tennessee, playing in his first professional golf tournament, tied for the 54-hole lead in the National Open here today with four amateurs, all from the University of Houston. Their score was 223, only 13 over par on historic old Baltus Oak, the course where Harry Vardon once tripped on a dining-room rug.

Best known of the Houston collegians was Rex Zark, who has been the Western, Trans-Miss, Southern, North-South, Broadmoor, British, and Idaho State amateur champion every year since the age of nine. The other talented members of the Texas team are Kermit Blank from Albany, New York, Babe Stimmett from Seattle, Washington, and Joel Wuthergrind from Worcester, Massachusetts.

None of the leaders could rest easily, it appeared, for only 16 strokes off the pace, poised to make one of his patented charges, was Arnold Palmer.

The championship was struck with an indelicate misfortune during Saturday's third round when R. J. "Bo" Mackey, the putt-putt pro, was disqualified on the first nine holes of his round. A USGA spokesman said Mackey had been warned repeatedly since Thursday to refrain from making obscene gestures and comments to women in his gallery but that he had refused to heed the warning. "We had no other course of action to take," said T. Philip Carter duPont Lawrence, a USGA vice president. "This, after all, is the Open championship. We're trying to identify the best golfer, not the crudest."

HOGAN WINS UNPRECEDENTED NINTH OPEN

OYSTER BISQUE, N.Y. — With the coveted National Open championship all but sewed up, Arnold Palmer caught his backswing in a flowering banyan today on historic old Baltus Oak, the course where Tommy Armour once bought lunch, and Ben Hogan, looking tanned and fit despite his eighty-one years, flashed past Palmer to capture his ninth Open title.

Palmer caught his swing in the tree at Baltus Oak's seventeenth hole and had to be rescued by a demolition team from the Corps of Engineers. Palmer was unable to complete the round and the tournament, and thus he will have to endure sectional qualifying again next year.

"It's pretty disheartening to know you can finish ten-ten and win, and then not even be able to play," said Palmer.

Hogan shot a flaming 67 in the final round for a 72-hole total of 301, only 21 over par. Hogan's round was the lowest since architect Robert Trent Jones had re-vamped Baltus Oak, placing a number of bunkers in the center of some tees and forcing carries of 280 yards or more over water.

There was a moment of pure drama at the final green after Hogan finished, flashing his familiar outgoing, quick-smiling expression. Hogan went over to Jones and shook his hand until the architect knelt down, ut-tering a bit of a whimper.

"I brought the monster to its knees," said Hogan.

Sam Snead, who mailed in his scores, again finished second.

None of the third-round leaders managed to finish.

Billy Tom Riddle, tormented by the sight of his first gallery, picked up at the third hole after striking his ball twenty-one times in a bunker. The entire University of Houston team, including Rex Zark, quit after nine and mysteriously departed for West Lafayette, Indiana, the site of next week's NCAA championships.

Greg Norman made another of his late-hour surges, and had a chance to tie, but he unwisely used a driver off the 72nd tee and hit it too far. The ball soared 357 yards, by most estimations, and not only out-of-bounds but over the marble statue of T. Philip Carter-Hughes Bentley duPont Lawrence, the man who built Baltus Oak.

As Hogan accepted the unprecedented ninth Open trophy in a moving ceremony near the eighteenth green, and in turn presented the USGA with his full set of clubs and his white cap for the Golf House museum, there were still thirty competitors out on the course, trying to complete the last nine holes in the dark.

Word briefly circulated that one of them, Frank Clack, an obscure driving range pro from Davenport, Iowa, could tie Hogan with two birdies over the last four holes, but USGA officials dismissed the news as malicious rumor.

In its only other action of the day, the USGA announced that the National Open of 2003 had been awarded to the Upper Course at historic old Baltus Oak, the club where Deane Beman first made love to a corporate logo.

Whoo-Ha, Arnie!

IT WAS, I still believe, the most remarkable day in golf since Mary Queen of Scots found herself three down to an unbathed bagpiper and invented the back nine. And now, given all these years of reflection, it still seems as significant as the day Arnold Palmer first hitched up his trousers, the moment Jack Nicklaus decided to lose weight and fluff-dry his hair, and that interlude in the pro shop when Ben Hogan selected his first white cap.

Small wonder that every sportswriter present, including myself, choked at the typewriter. It was simply too big, too wildly exciting, too crazily suspenseful, too suffocatingly dramatic for any of us to do it justice.

What exactly happened? Oh, not much. Just a routine collision of three decades at one historical intersection.

On that afternoon, in the span of just eighteen holes, we witnessed the arrival of Nicklaus, the coronation of Palmer, and the end of Hogan. Nicklaus was a twenty-year-old amateur who would own the 1970s. Palmer was a thirty-year-old pro who would dominate the 1960s.

Hogan was a forty-seven-year-old immortal who had overwhelmed the 1950s. While they had a fine supporting cast, it was primarily these three men who waged war for the U.S. Open championship on that Saturday of June 18, 1960. The battle was continuous, under a steaming Colorado sun at the Cherry Hills Country Club in Denver.

Things happened *to* them, *around* them.

Things happened in front of them, behind them.

Nobody knew where to go next, to see who had the lead, who was close, who had faltered.

Leader boards changed faster than stoplights.

And for a great while they were bleeding with red numbers.

In those days there was something known as Open Saturday. It is no longer part of golf—thanks to TV, no thanks, actually. But it was a day like no other; a day when the best golfers in the world were required to play 36 holes because it had always seemed to the USGA that a prolonged test of physical and mental stamina should go into the earning of the game's most important championship. Thus, Open Saturday lent itself to wondrous comebacks and funny collapses, and it provided a full day's ration of every emotion familiar to the athlete competing under pressure.

Open Saturday had been an institution with the USGA since its fourth championship in 1898, and there had been many a thriller before 1960, Saturdays that had tested the nerves and skill of the Bobby Joneses, the Gene Sarazens, the Walter Hagens, the Harry Vardons, the Byron Nelsons, the Sam Sneads, and, of course, the Ben Hogans.

But any serious scholar of the sport, or anyone fortunate enough to have been at Cherry Hills, is aware that the Open Saturday of Arnold, Jack, and Ben was extra special—a National Open that in meaning for the game continues to dwarf most of the others.

It was the Open in which Arnold Palmer shot a 65 in the last round and became the real Arnold Palmer. Threw his visor in the air, smoked a bunch of cigarettes, chipped in, drove a ball through a forest and onto a green, tucked in his shirttail, and lived happily ever after in the history books.

And that is pretty much what happened. But there is a constant truth about tournament golf: Other men have to lose a championship before one man can win it. And never has the final 18 of an Open produced as many losers as Cherry Hills did in 1960. When it was over, there were as many stretcher cases as there were shouts of "Whoo-ha, go get 'em, Arnie." And that stood to reason after you considered that in those insane four hours Palmer came from seven strokes off the lead and from fifteenth place to grab a championship he had never even been in contention for.

Palmer had arrived in Denver as the favorite. Two months earlier he had taken his second Masters with what was beginning to be known to the wire services as a "charge." He had almost been confirmed as the Player of the New Era, though not quite. But as late as noon on Open Saturday, after three rounds of competition, you would hardly have heard his name mentioned in Denver. A list of the leaders through 54 holes shows how hopeless his position seemed.

The scoreboard read:

> Mike Souchak 68-67-73—208
> Julius Boros 73-69-68—210
> Dow Finsterwald 71-69-70—210

Jerry Barber 69-71-70—210
Ben Hogan 75-67-69—211
Jack Nicklaus 71-71-69—211
Jack Fleck 70-70-72—212
Johnny Pott 75-68-69—212
Don Cherry 70-71-71—212
Gary Player 70-72-71—213
Sam Snead 72-69-73—214
Billy Casper 71-70-73—214
Dutch Harrison 74-70-70—214
Bob Shave 72-71-71—214
Arnold Palmer 72-71-72—215

Through Thursday's opening round, Friday's second round, and right up until the last hole of the first 18 on Saturday, this Open had belonged exclusively to Mike Souchak, a long-hitting, highly popular pro. His blazing total of 135 after 36 holes was an Open record. And as he stood on the eighteenth tee of Saturday's morning round, he needed only a par 4 for a 71 and a four-stroke lead on the field.

Then came an incident that gave everyone a foreboding about the afternoon. On Souchak's backswing, a camera clicked loudly. Souchak's drive soared out-of-bounds, and he took a double-bogey 6 for a 73. He never really recovered from the jolt. While the lead would remain his well into the afternoon, you could see Mike painfully allowing the tournament to slip away from him. He was headed for the slow death of a finishing 75 and another near-miss, like the one he had suffered the previous year in the Open at Winged Foot up in Westchester County.

Much has been written about Arnold in the locker room at Cherry Hills between rounds on Open Saturday. It has become a part of golfing lore. As it happened, I was there, one of two people with Arnold. The other was Bob Drum, a writer then with the Pittsburgh *Press*. It was a position that allowed Drum to enjoy the same close relationship with Palmer that the Atlanta *Journal's* O. B. Keeler once had with Bobby Jones.

Everybody had cheeseburgers and iced tea. We bathed our faces and arms with cold towels. It was too hot to believe that you could actually see snowcaps on the Rockies on the skyline.

As Palmer sat on the locker-room bench, there was no talk at all of who might win, only of how short and inviting the course was playing, of how Mike Souchak, with the start he had, would probably shoot 269 if the tournament were a Pensacola Classic instead of the Open.

Arnold was cursing the first hole at Cherry Hills, a 346-yard par 4 with an elevated tee. Three times he had just missed driving the green. As he left the group to join Paul Harney for their 1:42 starting time on the final 18, the thing on his mind was trying to drive that first green. It would be his one Cherry Hills accomplishment.

"If I drive the green and get a birdie or an eagle, I might shoot sixty-five," Palmer said. "What'll that do?"

Drum said, "Nothing. You're too far back."

"It would give me two-eighty," Palmer said. "Doesn't two-eighty always win the Open?"

"Yeah, when Hogan shoots it," I said, laughing heartily at my own wit.

Arnold lingered at the doorway, looking at us as if he were waiting for a better exit line.

"Go on, boy," Drum said. "Get out of here. Go make

your seven or eight birdies but shoot seventy-three. I'll see you later."

Bob Drum had been writing Palmer stories since Palmer was the West Pennsylvania amateur champion. On a Fort Worth newspaper, I had been writing Ben Hogan stories for ten years, but I had also become a friend of Palmer's because I was a friend of Drum's.

Palmer left the room but we didn't, for the simple reason that Mike Souchak, the leader, would not be starting his last round for another fifteen or twenty minutes. But the fun began before that. It started for us when word drifted back to the locker room that Palmer had indeed driven the first green and two-putted for a birdie. He had not carried the ball 346 yards in the air, but he had nailed it good enough for it to burn a path through the high weeds the USGA had nurtured in front of the green to prevent just such a thing from happening. Palmer had in fact barely missed his eagle putt from 20 feet.

Frankly, we thought nothing of it. Nor did we think much of the news that Arnold had chipped in from 35 feet for a birdie at the second. What *did* get Bob Drum's attention was the distant thunder which signaled that Arnold had birdied the third hole. He had wedged to within a foot of the cup.

We were standing near the putting green by the clubhouse, and we had just decided to meander out toward Souchak when Drum said, "Care to join me at the fourth hole?"

We broke into a downhill canter.

As we arrived at the green, Palmer was in the process of drilling an 18-foot birdie putt into the cup. He was now four under through four, two under for the championship, only three strokes behind Souchak, and there were a lot of holes left to play.

We stooped under the ropes at the fifth tee, as our armbands entitled us to, and awaited Arnold's entrance. He came in hitching up the pants and gazed down the fairway. Spotting us, he strolled over.

"Fancy seeing you here," he said with a touch of slyness.

Then he drank the rest of my Coke, smoked one of my cigarettes, and failed to birdie the hole, a par 5. On the other hand, he more than made up for it by sinking a curving 25-footer for a birdie at the par-3 sixth. At the seventh, he hit another splendid wedge to within six feet of the flag. He made the putt. And the cheers that followed told everybody on the golf course that Arnold Palmer had birdied six of the first seven holes.

It was history book stuff. And yet for all those heroics it was absolutely unreal to look up at a scoreboard out on the course and learn that Arnold Palmer still wasn't leading the Open. Some kid named Jack Nicklaus was. That beefy guy from Columbus paired with Hogan, playing two groups ahead of Palmer. The amateur. Out in 32. Five under now for the tournament.

Bob Drum sized up the scoreboard for everyone around him.

"The fat kid's five under and the whole world's four under," he said.

That was true one minute and not true the next. By the whole world, Drum meant Palmer, Hogan, Souchak, Boros, Fleck, Finsterwald, Barber, Cherry, etc. It was roughly 3:30 then, and for the next half hour it was impossible to know who was actually leading, coming on, falling back, or what. Palmer further complicated things by taking a bogey at the eighth. He parred the ninth and was out in a stinging 30, five under on the round. But in harsh truth, as I suggested to Bob Drum at the time, he was still only three under for the tournament and two strokes off the pace of Nicklaus or Boros or Souchak—possibly all three. And God knows, I said, what Hogan, Fleck, and Cherry—not to mention Dutch Harrison, or even Ted Kroll—were doing while we were standing there talking.

Dutch Harrison, for example, had gone out very early and was working on a 69 and 283. And way back behind even Palmer was Ted Kroll, who had begun the round at 216, one stroke worse off than Palmer. Kroll and Jack Fleck had put almost the same kind of torch to Cherry Hills' front nine holes that Palmer had. Kroll had birdied five of the first seven holes, with one bogey included. Fleck had birdied five of the first six, also with a bogey included. Kroll was going to wind up firing the second-best round of the day, a 67, which would pull him into what later would look like a 200-way tie for third place at the popular figure of 283.

Meanwhile, we were out on the course thinking about Palmer's chances in all of this when Drum made his big pronouncement of the day.

"My man's knocked 'em all out," he said. "They just haven't felt the shock waves yet."

History has settled for Bob Drum's analysis, and perhaps that is the truth of the matter after all. The story of the 1960 Open has been compressed into one sentence: Arnold Palmer birdied six of the first seven holes and won.

But condensations kill. What is missing is everything that happened after four o'clock. The part about Mike Souchak losing the lead for the first time only after he bogied the ninth hole. The part about Nicklaus blowing the lead he held all by himself when he took three ghastly putts from only 10 feet at the thirteenth. This was the first real indication that they were all coming back to Palmer now, for Nicklaus's bogey dropped him into a four-way tie with Palmer, Boros, and Fleck.

But so much more is still missing from the condensation. Nicklaus's woeful inexperience as a young amateur cost him another three-putt bogey at the fourteenth hole, and so, as suddenly as he had grabbed the lead, he was out of it. Then it was around 4:45 and Palmer was sharing the lead with Hogan and Fleck, each of them four under. But like Nicklaus, Fleck would leave it on the greens. Boros had started leaving it on the greens and in the bunkers somewhat earlier. He was trapped at the fourteenth and eighteenth, for instance, and in between he blew a three-footer. In the midst of all this, Palmer was playing a steady back side of one birdie and eight pars on the way to completing his 65. And until the last two holes of the championship, the only man who had performed more steadily than Palmer, or seemed to be enduring the Open stress with as much steel as he, was—no surprise—Ben Hogan.

It was getting close to five-thirty when Hogan and Palmer were alone at four under par in the championship, and the two of them, along with everybody else— literally everyone on the golf course—had somehow wound up on the seventeenth hole, the 71st of the tournament.

The seventeenth at Cherry Hills is still a long, straightaway par-5 of 548 yards, with a green fronted by a pond. In 1960 it was a drive, a layup, and a pitch. And there they all were. Hogan and Nicklaus contemplating their pitch shots as the twosome of Boros and

Player waited to hit their second shots, while the two-some of Palmer and Paul Harney stood back on the tee.

Hogan was faced with a delicate shot of about 50 yards to a pin sittting altogether too close to the water, on the front of the green, to try anything risky. Ben had hit 34 straight greens in regulation that Saturday. He needed only to finish with two pars for a 69 and a total of 280—and nobody understood better than Hogan what it meant to reach the clubhouse first with a good score in a major.

Armed with all this knowledge, I knelt in the rough and watched Hogan address the shot and said brilliantly to Drum, "He probably thinks he needs a birdie with Arnold behind him, but I'll guarantee you one thing—he'll be over the water."

At which point Hogan hit the ball in the water.

It was a foot shy of perfect, but it hit the bank and spun back in.

He made a bogey 6. And in trying to erase that misfortune on the eighteenth with a huge drive, which might conceivably produce a birdie, he hooked his tee shot into the lake and suffered a triple bogey 7. Sadly, only thirty minutes after he had been a co-leader with just two holes to go, Hogan finished in a tie for ninth place, four strokes away.

Second place then was left to the twenty-year-old with the crew cut, and Nicklaus's score of 282 remains the lowest total ever posted by an amateur in the Open.

All in all, these were tremendous performances by an aging Hogan and a young Nicklaus. The two of them had come the closest to surviving Palmer's shock waves.

It was later on, back in the locker room, long after Palmer had slung his visor in the air for the photographers, that Ben Hogan said the truest thing of all about the day. Ben would know best.

He said, "I guess they'll say I lost it. Well, one more foot and the wedge on seventeen would have been perfect. But I'll tell you something. I played thirty-six holes today with a kid who should have won this Open by ten shots."

Jack Nicklaus would start winning Opens and other major titles soon enough as a pro, of course. But wasn't it nice to have Arnold around first?

The Dream Tournament

EVEN EVERYONE in the normally blasé pressroom was excited when the World "Dream World" Invitational got under way at charming old Pine Oak Merionhurst Country Club in Old Charming, New York, the first course Donald Ross forgot to name for an Indian tribe, and the 418th golf course he designed on the menu of a railroad dining car.

Just to glance at the first-round pairings was a thrill, for every competitor had to have won at least three majors to be invited—that was the strict rule of the tournament's creator and director, Baltus Jenkins-Foot, the tireless golf historian and recent inventor of the long-shafted jumbo wedge, a club of considerable value when playing a golf hole bordered by a Florida swamp.

Indeed, the pairings sheet read like a Who's Who of the niblick crowd. To wit:

10:30—Harry Vardon, J. H. Taylor, James Braid.
10:37—Tommy Armour, Lawson Little, Bobby Locke.

10:44—Jimmy Demaret, Lee Trevino, Raymond Floyd.
10:51—Bobby Jones, Walter Hagen, Gene Sarazen.
10:58—Jack Nicklaus, Arnold Palmer, Gary Player.
11:05—Ben Hogan, Byron Nelson, Sam Snead.
11:12—Tom Watson, Seve Ballesteros, Nick Faldo.
11:19—Billy Casper, Hale Irwin, Denny Shute.
11:26—Cary Middlecoff, Ralph Guldahl, Julius Boros.

A small but glittering field of twenty-seven. Not a bad seed in the bunch, observed the tournament director proudly. He went on to say the field might have been larger were it not for two reasons: (1) The exclusive course, Pine Oak Merionhurst, needed to be clear for members' play by noon each day, and (2) the other golfers who had won at least three majors and might have been invited were, in fact, rejected because they never should have won three majors in the first place, if you wanted his personal opinion on the matter.

"But I can tell you," the tournament director said, "that it was a close call between Denny Shute and Henry Cotton."

A word about the course. It was a leafy, shady, creek-infested layout with numerous old-fashioned blind shots and postage-stamp greens. It was short, only 6,413 yards with a par of 70, but could play much longer if members happened to not be using some of the elegant fairways for croquet.

This was the first event ever staged at Pine Oak Merionhurst. The club had once scheduled an exhibition match back in 1929 between Bobby Jones and Mary Pickford but it had been abruptly canceled due to the Wall Street crash, which took the lives of seventeen despondent members, all of whom drowned themselves in the rushing stream to the left of the sixteenth, the short hole.

A simple bronze plaque, similar to those at the Augusta National, marks the spot. The inscription says:

"HERE PERISHED ONE-FIFTH OF THE WEALTH OF AMERICA ON OCT. 29, 1929, THANKS TO THAT IDIOT HERBERT HOOVER."

The tournament director felt the need to explain a couple more things about his creative pairings before Harry Vardon hit the first ball.

Inserting the Bobby Jones, Ben Hogan, and Jack Nicklaus groups in the middle of the pack, he admitted, was purely an accommodation for DNQ-TV, the cable network that was covering the event on Thursday and Friday, before ABC took over the last two rounds.

This would enable the deft producer of the cable telecast to show brief glimpses of Jones, Hogan, and Nicklaus—the only three golfers he had ever heard of—during idle moments of an equestrian competition in Hamburg, Germany.

Further, the tournament director complimented himself on wisely putting Cary Middlecoff, Ralph Guldahl, and Julius Boros in the last group on Thursday. Each was penalized four strokes for slow play and they were never a threat in the championship.

Guldahl stopped once too often to comb his long black hair as he strolled from a bunker to a green.

Boros pulled up so many weeds to chew on he actually widened the third, seventh, and twelfth fairways.

And the pause at the top of Middlecoff's backswing with his driver was clocked once at 5 minutes 37 seconds.

Byron Nelson's one-under 69 led the first round, thanks in large part to Sam Snead's disastrous 8 at the last hole. Sam mistook the par-5 eighteenth at Pine Oak Merionhurst for a par 3 and hit a 9-iron off the tee, which failed to clear the quarry. After that, most agreed, Snead's 8 wasn't such a bad score.

"Somebody might have told me what par was," Sam said sullenly when he was interviewed later.

Nelson looked exhausted and apologized for the 69, the highest round he had shot in seven months. He was coming off eleven straight tournament victories and had been playing with great confidence until he arrived at Pine Oak Merionhurst and was somewhat demoralized to learn from a golf statistician that the total purses of his entire career wouldn't move him ahead of Tommy Aaron on the all-time money list.

"It's enough to make a man want to retire and become a cattle rancher," Byron said.

In second place with a very fortunate and rather controversial 71 was Gary Player, who was allowed fourteen free drops in the woods because of TV cables, and salvaged par on each occasion.

Gary said Pine Oak Merionhurst was the finest golf course of its type he'd ever seen, and he liked his position and his chances for the twelfth Grand Slam of his career. He reminded the pressroom that coming into the World "Dream World" Invitational he had previously won the opens of Luxembourg, Helsinki, and Dar es Salaam, and unlike Jack Nicklaus, he had just stepped off a fourteen-hour flight from Johannesburg.

Jones, Hogan, and Nicklaus all got in with 72s, but in different ways. Hogan three-putted seven times, Nicklaus flubbed two pitching wedges from the center of the fairway, and Jones called four penalty shots on himself, convinced that his ball moved half a rotation as he addressed various chip shots.

Walter Hagen posted a 73, a score deemed sort of miraculous, considering that he played in a tuxedo and suffered several sneezing fits from stopping to smell so many flowers.

All others shot 73 or 74 with the notable exceptions of Vardon, Taylor, and Braid, who almost suffocated luggng around sixteen British Open titles in their heavy tweed suits. They shot 77, 78, and 81, respectively, but thoroughly entertained their triumvirate of pipe-smoking fans, who parked their Triumvirates in the patrons' lot and took a shuttle bus to the course.

Vardon held a press conference after his round at which he primarily complimented Americans on their air-conditioning.

"The criminal classes seem to have made some progress since my last visit," the Englishman said, "although the tea in the clubhouse could use a bit of strength, and I could say a word or two about this thing you call—Velveeta, is it? Sorry that chap Ouimet is not here, by the way, I was rather looking forward to having another go at him."

Friday was the day Gene Sarazen holed out the first of his astounding double eagles with his 4-wood shot to the fifteenth. The shot was all the more remarkable considering that this second over the pond had only been a three-quarter 5-iron for everyone else in the field.

The double eagle helped Sarazen get in with a 68 and the 36-hole lead at 142, thanks in large part to Sam Snead's disastrous 8 at the last hole. Sam used a driver off the tee this time but smacked the ball so far it reached the second quarry.

"Somebody might have told me the wind was with me," Sam said sullenly.

Seve Ballesteros fired a harrowing round of 69, extracting his tee shots from seven parking lots and three concession stands, saving par each time. His total of 143 put him in second place, but he wasn't happy.

"The wind, the sand, the trees, the water," Ballesteros said, gesturing furiously. "The greens, the food, the hotel, the caddie, the wife . . ."

There was a four-way tie for third place at 144 involving the three favorites—Jones, Hogan, and Nicklaus—plus the first-day leader, Byron Nelson.

Nelson slipped to a 75, the highest round he had shot since he was three years old. An old stomach disorder that cropped up may have been to blame for his spotty play. On the other hand, it may have had something to do with Byron's being informed overnight that he had now fallen behind Scott Hoch on the all-time money list.

Jones, Hogan, and Nicklaus all shot 72s again, but in different ways.

Hogan three-putted five greens and seemed outwardly perturbed by two things, not the least of which were all of the nonsmokers in his gallery who kept fanning themselves and groaning as Ben persistently lit up.

Another annoyance was the Hollywood director-writer who dogged him all the way around, hoping to get his approval to do a sequel to *Follow the Sun,* the title of which would be *Honey, I Shrunk the Par 5s.*

Jones called another penalty stroke on himself when two manuscripts fell from his arms and accidentally moved his ball as he stood over a putt at the twelfth. One manuscript was a novel he was editing for Sinclair Lewis, and the other was a scientific formula he was working on with Albert Einstein.

"Bob's intellect doesn't usually get in his way," Hogan whispered to a friend in the gallery.

Nicklaus had made but one birdie in two days and attributed this to the poor design of the course.

"The greens are where the tees should be in most cases," Jack said. "It's nothing that can't be fixed, however, and I will be happy to work with the club on the changes if the membership is willing to invest the $22 million it will take to do it right."

Gary Player, who had been second after Thursday's round, was among the withdrawals on Friday.

Despite the 95-degree temperature, Gary was dressed all in black—black cap, black shirt, black pants, "to hold in the heat," he explained—and he actually started to melt as he stood on the roof of the clubhouse and argued about a ruling for half an hour.

Denied the free drop, Player quit. "There goes the Slam," he said sadly, as officials watched his left leg becoming an ink stain.

The threesome of Tommy Armour, Lawson Little, and Bobby Locke went into the Men's Grill for a drink at the turn and never came out again.

Hale Irwin walked off at the eighth, complaining that Pine Oak Merionhurst was too easy. "I can only play well on tough golf courses," he said.

The long-range forecast for clear weather forced Billy Casper's withdrawal. He was, after all, the only player in the field who had won all three of his majors on the day after the tournaments should have ended, owing to a thunderstorm at Winged Foot and playoffs at Augusta and Olympic.

Raymond Floyd dropped out after being bothered by a variety of outside influences. For one thing, there was Jimmy Demaret's constant singing, and for another, there was Lee Trevino's constant joke telling. Then came the news that his home near Miami had caught fire again, although the flames had quickly been extinguished by the arrival of Hurricane Duane.

"If it's not one thing, it's another," Raymond said, packing his bag, "but fortunately, I expect to win fifty-six tournaments on the senior tour."

The departure of Denny Shute was understandable. He simply grew weary of having to explain to the crowd who he was and why he was there.

"I guess winning two PGAs and a British Open doesn't mean much to a New York cabdriver," he said. "Fine. They want to see Greg Norman, let 'em go to Doral."

Saturday was a day of considerable excitement. Jones and Nicklaus each shot 68 to share the 54-hole lead at 212, thanks in large part to Sam Snead's disastrous 8 at the final hole. Sam negotiated the quarries safely but then five-putted the green.

"Somebody might have told me it was downhill and fast," Sam said sullenly.

Hogan was a stroke back with his 69 and might have been tied for the lead if he hadn't three-putted the eighteenth, having missed a tap-in when he was distracted by the voices from a TV tower.

Ben couldn't help overhearing ABC's Steve Melnyk dropping tidbits of misinformation, such as the fact that his center-shaft brass putter had never been part of a doorknob that was stolen by Ky Laffoon from Al Capone's home in Key Biscayne, Florida, the generally accepted legend, but instead had been carved from King Arthur's sword by an old club maker in Musselburgh.

Over the putt, Hogan was also disturbed by Brent

Musburger's confused references to "Bantam Bob Jones" and "Slammin' Lord Sarazen, the Wee Haigmon."

Sarazen, the 36-hole leader, holed out another 4-wood shot for a double eagle at the fifteenth, but this couldn't make up for the penalty shots he was assessed for carrying too many clubs in his bag, half of them hickory, half of them steel.

"It's a little hard to know what to use when you don't know what decade you're in," Sarazen said testily.

Seve Ballesteros rapidly took himself out of contention on Saturday at the second hole. That's where he lost his ball after a wild tee shot into an area of hospitality tents. In fact, he not only lost his ball but his entire bag of clubs, his caddie, and his entourage of a dozen Spaniards, all of whom claimed to be his brothers, cousins, and financial managers, and had been audibly arguing among themselves for three days.

Ballesteros, paired with Tom Watson and Nick Faldo, was part of the most amusing threesome of the day. Essentially, they played three onesomes. When the fast-moving Watson would be putting out on the green. Seve would be back down the fairway, addressing another trouble shot with one foot on a bulkhead and the other foot on the edge of a rowboat. Meanwhile, Faldo would still be back on the tee, methodically practicing his takeaway and waiting for a call from David Leadbetter on his cellular phone.

Up to now, Arnold Palmer, the overwhelming favorite, hadn't caused much of a stir. Arnold had pleased his rowdy fans by driving through and around several clumps of trees and holing long putts for pars and bogeys, but he was 15 over par after shooting three rounds of 74, 75, and 76.

"It's nothing a little fifty-five won't cure," Arnold said, still confident.

The first hole had been bugging Palmer. It was a relatively short, downhill par 4. He had been trying to slash his tee shot all the way to the green, but the waist-high rough that had been purposely grown in front of the green had stopped his ball all three days.

He said, "If I could drive the first green and two-putt for a birdie. I could shoot 55. That would give me two-eighty. Doesn't two-eighty always win the World 'Dream World' Invitational?"

His audience of sportswriters in the locker room could only react with bewilderment, inasmuch as this was the first World "Dream World" Invitational ever held.

Sunday's final round exploded with drama in all directions, but first, here is how the huge leader board on the clubhouse veranda read before play began:

Bobby Jones	72-72-68	212
Jack Nicklaus	72-72-68	212
Ben Hogan	72-72-69	213
Byron Nelson	69-75-70	214
Sam Snead	73-69-73	215
Walter Hagen	73-73-70	216
Gene Sarazen	74-68-74	216
Tom Watson	73-74-71	218
Lee Trevino	74-73-71	218
Deane Beman	77-71-70	218

The mysterious appearance of Deane Beman's name on the leader board was an obvious prank, and a staff person from *Golf Digest* immediately confessed to it. The tournament director, Baltus Jenkins-Foot, enjoyed a good laugh along with everyone else, but then had the name replaced by that of Harry Vardon.

Vardon had fought back bravely after the first day with rounds of 71 and 70, principally because he had adjusted to the heat by shedding his tweeds and necktie, but when he first showed up on the tee in his baseball cap, knit shirt, and Bermuda shorts, Taylor and Braid were mortified.

"What about that, then?" Taylor said, glancing at Braid.

"Good grief!" said Braid. "He looks like a bloody tourist at Disney World. Sauce for the tabs, if I've a mind."

Byron Nelson scorched the front nine with seven birdies and seemed to take an insurmountable lead, but then he lapsed into a string of bogeys after learning that eighteen victories in one year would still leave him behind Jodie Mudd on the all-time money list.

Walter Hagen, between sneezes, and still wearing a tuxedo, got off to a good start with two birdies, but suddenly picked up and joined a black-tie party on the lawn of a castle parallel to the third fairway.

"Aren't you a contender?" the host asked.

"No problem," Hagen said. "I've never won a major Bobby Jones played in."

"Oh?" the host said. "Well, make yourself at home, by all means. The bar's over there—and Demaret's dropping by to sing shortly."

Arnold Palmer's hordes were ecstatic when he finally drove the first green, a blow of 341 yards, though it was with the aid of a sprinkler head, a bounce off a stone path, and an overzealous fan named Howdy throwing the ball the last 50 yards.

Palmer's army grew by the thousands as he birdied

the first four holes, but his hopes for a 55 were dashed at the fifth when he hooked his drive into the deep rough. He gallantly tried to hit a driver out of the rough but found a bunker. He gallantly tried to play a 1-iron out of the steep-walled bunker. He gallantly tried to play a 3-iron out of the same bunker. He gallantly played a sand wedge out of the same bunker, backward, eventually reached the green with a screaming 3-wood and drew a mighty roar when he sank a 60-foot putt for a 7. The hole seemed to sum up his entire career.

Arnold's adoring crowd would have stayed with him all the way, regardless of what he might shoot, but the fifth was near the private airstrip where his plane was waiting and he took off.

Watson and Trevino each chipped in a half dozen times for birdies, but neither could chip in quite enough to compensate for the bogeys that would result when the chip shots would miss the flagsticks and dart across the greens into bunkers and water hazards. Trevino was last seen changing his shoes in the parking lot and saying he never should have come to Pine Oak Merion-hurst in the first place.

Gene Sarazen coasted along content with pars, staying near the lead, feeling confident that he could hole out another 4-wood shot at the fifteenth. He did exactly that, except that he caught the shot on the toe and it wound up in the cup on the adjacent thirteenth green. Sportswriters found it hard to recall a double eagle that had been more costly.

Sam Snead blew the tournament once and for all, thanks in large part to a disastrous 8 on the 72nd hole. Informed that he only needed a 6 to win and a 7 to tie, Snead chose to play safe, going up the fairway of Pine

Oak Merionhurst's Lower Course. Naturally, he incurred a rash of penalty strokes.

"Somebody might have told me it was out-of-bounds," Sam said sullenly.

The championship was decided over the final nine holes by the three immortals who were paired together, Bobby Jones, Ben Hogan, and Jack Nicklaus. Certainly every writer on hand of a mature age expected this to be the case.

They were all tied for the lead going to the tenth, but that's where Jones called a needless penalty shot on himself. "That's a force of habit," explained O. B. Keeler, who was among a group of journalists walking inside the ropes.

"He doesn't need too many of those," a writer from Texas said. "He's not playing Eugene Homans today."

Jones climbed back into a share of the lead with Hogan and Nicklaus when his second shot at the fifteenth skipped across the water and he sank a curling 12-foot putt for a birdie.

"Is his putter really nicknamed Calamity Jane?" someone asked O. B. Keeler.

"I made it up." Keeler shrugged.

There was little conversation between the immortals, but as the three men stood on the sixteenth green Jones remarked to Hogan that he was keenly awed by Nicklaus's power.

"Nicklaus plays a game with which I am not familiar," Jones added.

"You're away," said Hogan, reaching for a cigarette.

It came down to this: Nicklaus hit a 1-iron to the lip of the cup at the seventeenth for the birdie that got him in with a 68. Jones holed another 12-footer on the eighteenth for the par that got *him* in with a 68. Hogan, hitting every fairway and every green in regulation, birdied the sixteenth and eighteenth holes for a 67, low round of the tournament.

They all tied at 280 and were declared co-champions, basically because they refused for various reasons to enter into an 18-hole playoff the next day.

Jones was already overdue in Hollywood to start filming a series of golfing short subjects with Frank Lloyd Wright and Sigmund Freud.

Nicklaus was eager to leave and put the finishing touches on Kempernole, a public course he had designed for a strange sect of insurance men living on a reservation near Chicago. Besides, that's where the PGA was being held next week and Jack's sons had all received exemptions.

Hogan discovered that the 1-iron had been stolen out of his bag, but this had nothing to do with his refusal to play.

"I brought the monster to its knees once," he said. "What do you want from me?"

The Glory Game
at Goat Hills

Goat Hills is gone now. It was swallowed up by the bulldozers of progress, and in the end it was nice to know that something could take a divot out of those fairways. But all of the regulars had left long before. I suppose it will be all right to talk about it now, about the place and the people and the times we had. Maybe it will explain why I don't play golf so much anymore. It's swell to get invited to play Winged Dip and Burning Foot and all those fancy clubs where they have real flagsticks instead of broom handles, but I usually beg off. Frankly, I'm still over-golfed from all those years at Goat Hills in Texas. You would be too if . . . well, let me tell you some of it. I'll try to be truthful and not too sentimental, but where shall I begin? With Cecil? Why not? He was sort of a symbol in those days, and . . .

WE CALLED HIM Cecil the Parachute because he fell down a lot. He would attack the golf ball with a whining, leaping move—more of a calisthenic than a swing—and occasionally, in his spectacular struggles for extra distance, he would soar right off the end of elevated tees.

He was a slim, bony, red-faced little man who wore crepe-soled shoes and a heavily starched shirt that crackled when he marked his ball, always inching it forward as much as possible. When he was earthbound, Cecil drove a truck for Grandma's Cookies, and he always parked it behind a tall hedge near the clubhouse, out of sight of passing cars, one of which might have Grandma in it.

Anyhow, when the truck was there, you could be pretty sure that not only was Cecil out on the course but so, most likely, were Tiny, Easy, Magoo, and Foot the Free, Ernie, Matty, Rush, and Grease Repellent, Little Joe, Weldon the Oath, Jerry, John the Band-Aid, and Moron Tom—and me. I was known as Dump, basically because of what so many partners thought I did to them for money.

There would be an excellent chance that all of us would be in one hollering, protesting, arguing, club-slinging gangsome, betting huge sums of money we didn't have. In other words, when Cecil's truck was hidden behind the hedge, you knew the game was on.

The game was not the kind the United States Golf Association would have approved of, but it was the kind we played for about fifteen years at a windy, dusty, seldom mowed, stone-hard, practically treeless, residentially surrounded public course named Worth Hills in Fort Worth, Texas.

Goat Hills we called it, not too originally.

It was a gambling game that went on in some form or other, involving anywhere from three to twenty-two players, almost every day of every year when a lot of us were younger and bored silly. The game not only survived my own shaft-breaking, divot-stomping, club-slinging presence, it outlasted rain, snow, heat, wars, tornadoes, jobs, studies, illnesses, divorces, births, deaths, romances, and pinball machines.

Nearly all of the days at the Hills began the same way. Some of us would be slouched in wicker chairs on the small front porch of the wooden clubhouse, smoking, drinking coffee or Cokes, complaining about worldly things, such as why none of the movie houses in town had changed features in five or six weeks, and why most of the girls we knew only wanted to hump rich guys—didn't they care anything about debonair?

Say it was August. We would be looking across the putting green and into the heat. In Texas in the summer, you can see the heat. It looks like germs. In fact, say it was the day of the Great Cart Wreck.

There on the porch, Matty, who had a crew cut and wore glasses, was playing tunes on his uppr front teeth with his fingernails. He had learned how to do this in study hall in high school, and for money he could play almost any tune, including "Sixty-Minute Man" and "Saber Dance," and you could actually recognize it.

I was reading a book of some kind as usual. Something light by a Russian or a German.

Tiny, a heavyset railroad conductor, came out of the clubhouse in his flaming red shirt and red slacks, and said, "Dump, what you gonna do with all that book crap in your head?"

"None of it stays there," I said.

Foot the Free, which was short for Big Foot the Freeloader, was practice-putting at a chipped-out crevice in the concrete, a spot that marked the finish of the greatest single hole I've ever seen played—but more about that later.

Little Joe was out on the putting green, trying to perfect a stroke behind his back, a trick shot, in the hope that somebody would one day suggest a behind-the-back putting contest.

Magoo was sitting next to me on the porch.

"Anything about God in that book?" he asked.

"Some."

"Anything in there about what God did to me on the back nine yesterday?"

Around the corner came John the Band-Aid, cleats on, clubs over his shoulder, handkerchief around his neck, impatient as always.

"You, you, you, and you, and you too," he said. "All of you two, two, two, automatic one-down presses, get-evens on nine and eighteen. Whipsaw everybody seventy or better for five."

We began tying our golf shoes.

John the Band-Aid removed three clubs from his bag, dropped the bag on the gravel, and started swinging the clubs in a violent limbering-up exercise.

"Me and Little Joe got all teams for five match and five medal—dollar cats and double on birdies," he said.

Little Joe, who played without a shirt and had a blond ducktail, said, "Damn, John, I'd sure like to pick my own partner someday. You gonna play good or scrape it around like yesterday?"

John the Band-Aid said, "Well, you can have some of *me*, if it'll keep your interest up."

"I try five," said Little Joe in his high-pitched voice. "Five and a R-ra C."

Little Joe and I took a cart. So did John and Magoo. We had won money the day before, so we could afford to ride. The others walked, carrying their own clubs. We were an eightsome, but others would no doubt join us along the way. It wasn't unusual for other players to drive their cars around the course, find the game, hop out, and get it on.

It was Matty one afternoon who drove his red Olds right up to the edge of the third green, jumped out with his golf shoes and glove already on, and said, "Do I have a duck in the car?" He had driven straight to the game from the University of Oklahoma, a distance of some two hundred miles, and he had the duck in the car in case somebody wanted to bet him he didn't have a live duck in the car.

We played the first eight holes and then came the long interlude of bookkeeping on the ninth tee.

John the Band-Aid had earned his nickname by bleeding a lot, such as he did this day because he had shot even par but was losing to everybody. Which was why he had teed up his ball first—the game worked in reverse etiquette.

"All right, Magoo," he said, "you got me out, out, even, even, one down, and one down. I press your young ass for ten. Foot, you got me out, out, out, and one down. You're pushed for eight. Window closed?"

And so it went.

The ninth tee at Goat Hills was on a bluff, above a steep dropoff into a cluster of hackberry trees, a creek, rocks, and weeds. It was a par 4. The drive had to carry the ravine, and if you could hit it far enough, you had about a 7-iron to the green, going back toward the clubhouse.

John the Band-Aid tightened his straw hat and dug in for the tee shot.

"I'm gonna hit this summitch to Dallas," he said.

"Outhit you for five," Magoo said.

"You're on. Anybody else?"

"I try five," Little Joe said.

"You're on."

John the Band-Aid then curved a wondrous slice into the right rough, and coming off his follow-through, he slung his driver in the general direction of Eagle Mountain Lake, which was thirty miles behind us.

He just missed hitting Little Joe, who was nimble enough to dance out of the way.

Little Joe said, "Man, they ought to put you in a box and take you to the World's Fair."

John's arms were folded and he was staring off in an aimless direction, burning inside. Suddenly, then, he dashed over to his bag, jerked out his 2-iron, and slung it against the water fountain, snapping the shaft in half.

"That club cost me a shot on the fourth," he explained.

I wasn't all that happy myself. One under and no money ahead. Maybe that's why I pointed the three-wheel electric cart straight down the hill, full speed ahead, a getaway cart.

Over the rocks and ditches we went darting, and that's when the front wheel struck a large stone in the creek bed. All I recall hearing was Little Joe's voice.

"Son of a young . . . !"

We both went over the front end, headfirst, the bags and clubs flying out over and behind us.

I guess I was knocked out for ten seconds. When I came to, the cart was pinning down my left leg, battery acid was eating away at my shirt, and broken clubs were everywhere.

Little Joe was sitting down in the rocks examining his skinned elbows, and giggling.

The others were standing around, looking down at

us, considering whether to lift the cart off my leg, or leave me there to lose all bets.

Magoo glanced at Little Joe's white canvas bag which was already being eaten into by battery acid.

"Two dollars says Joe don't have a bag by the four-teenth," Magoo said.

My ankle was swollen. I had to take off my shoe and play the rest of the round in one shoe.

It is a remarkable footnote in golfing history that I birdied that ninth hole, to which Matty said, "I done been beat by everything now. Dead man comes out of the creek and makes a birdie."

Little Joe's bag lasted exactly until the fourteenth hole. After holing out a putt, he went to pick it up but there was nothing left but the two metal rings and a shoulder strap.

And most of his left trouser leg was going fast.

"Two says Joe is stark naked by the seventeenth," Magoo said.

That day, Little Joe and I both managed birdies on the eighteenth, winning all presses and get-evens, and Magoo and John the Band-Aid talked for weeks about the time they got beat by a cripple and a guy who was on fire.

On other days at the Hills, purely out of boredom, we played the course backward, or to every other hole, or every third hole, or entirely out of bounds except for the greens, which meant you had to stay in the roads and lawns. We also played the course with only one club, or just two clubs, and sometimes at night.

One game we invented was the Thousand-Yard Dash.

This was a one-hole marathon that started on the far-thest point on the course from the clubhouse—beside the twelfth green—and ended at the chipped-out crevice in the concrete on the clubhouse porch.

I'm not quite sure, but I think this game was the brainchild of either Foot the Free, Matty, or me. We had once played through six blocks of downtown Fort Worth, from Seventh Street to the courthouse, mostly on Commerce Street, without getting arrested.

On the day of the first Thousand-Yard Dash, some of us went to the left of the rock outhouse perched atop the highest point on the course, and some played to the right of it. I followed Foot the Free because he could never afford to lose—he carried the same five-dollar bill in his pocket for about eight years.

We hooked a driver, hooked another driver, hooked a third driver, then hooked a spoon—you had to hook the ball to get distance at Goat Hills—and this got us within a pitching wedge of the porch.

Most of the other twelve were out of it by now, lost in creeks or the flower beds of apartment houses bordering the first fairway.

My approach shot carried the porch, slammed against a wall of the clapboard clubhouse, chased Wells Howard, the pro, inside the front door, and brought a scream from Lola, his wife and bookkeeper. The ball came to rest about twenty feet from the crevice and was puttable, if I moved a chair.

Foot played a bounce shot at the porch. He lofted a high wedge, let it bounce off the gravel. It hopped up over the curb, skidded against a wall, and stopped about 10 feet from the crevice.

We borrowed a broom from Lola and swept dirt particles out of our putting lines.

The other players gathered around to make side bets.

Two rent-club players came out of the clubhouse and stepped in our lines.

"Hey!" I said to them. "This is business!"

"Smart-ass punks," one of them mumbled.

I gave my putt too good a rap. It went past the crevice and wound up in a row of pull carts at the end of the porch.

"Unnatural hazard," I said. "Free drop."

An instantly formed rules committee consisting of Magoo, Matty, and Grease Repellent, who worked at a Texaco station, basically decided that my request was bullshit.

I had to play it out of the pull carts, which was why I eighteen-putted for a 23.

Against anyone else, I might have still had a chance, but Foot was one of the great putters in history, on any kind of surface. If anything, the concrete looked like bent to Foot compared to the texture of the gnarled Bermuda greens out on the course.

He calmly tapped his 10-footer and it wobbled slowly, slowly, slowly over the concrete, wavered, and went in!

That was one of the two greatest holes I ever saw played. The other was when my friend Bud Shrake made a 517 on a five-block hole that stretched from Goat Hills' first tee to a brown leather loafer in another friend's apartment.

The longest hole we ever played was from the first tee at Goat Hills to the third green at Colonial Country Club, roughly fifteen blocks away.

The first time we played it, Rush's dad, a retired oilman, caddied for him in a black Lincoln, and Cecil got bit by a cocker spaniel.

Playing through neighborhoods required a unique shot, we discovered. A blade putter was an ideal club to keep the ball low so it would get extra roll on the pavement.

Some of us went down Stadium Drive, past the TCU football stadium, then left on Park Hill and over the houses. Others went the back way, down Alton Road.

I happened to have sliced a blade putter into a bed of irises on Alton Road and was looking for it when I saw Cecil down the driveway.

He was contemplating a shot that would have to rise quickly to clear a cyclone fence, then duck sharply under an oak, then hook severely to get around a tile roof, and then slice to land in the street.

As Cecil studied the shot, a dog was barking at his ankles.

Cecil leaped at the ball in his customary manner and drove the ball straight into the fence, about eight feet in front of him, and his follow-through carried him forward and onto the ground on his elbows and stomach. He slid into the fence, and the spaniel chased after him as if it were retrieving a sock.

Cecil scrambled to his feet and tiptoed back down the driveway, and withdrew from the competition.

"Hurried the shot," he said. "That sucker was growlin' at me, and just when I started to swing, I seen a lady cussin' me through the kitchen window."

Tiny quit at a fishpond. Grease Repellent lost his ball when he struck a sundial. Easy Reid met a fellow and stopped to sell him some insurance. John the Band-Aid broke his blade putter when he sailed it at a chimney. Foot and Magoo were the only two who finished, and they had to play out fast after they climbed over the Colonial fence because some members sent a caddie back to the clubhouse to get the club manager, who would, in turn, call the police.

There was an argument about who won, and a playoff was decided upon. Magoo wanted to play back to Goat Hills, to the cold-drink box in the lunchroom. Foot wanted to play to Herb Massey's Cafe, about three miles away, to the third leg of the shuffle-bowl machine. Herb's was where Matty once showed up one day with his shirt and pants on backward, and his glasses on the back of his head, and posted a score of 280 on the shuffle bowl, sliding the puck backward.

Foot and Magoo wound up splitting the money, and we all went back to Goat Hills and got in a putting game that lasted until midnight.

Why we did such things was because we lived in Fort Worth, the town that gave you Ben Hogan and Byron Nelson, and offered little else to do.

Besides, it was Texas.

Golf had always received lavish attention in the newspapers, and it was at a very early age that you knew about Hogan and Nelson and others: Jimmy Demaret, Lloyd Mangrum, Ralph Guldahl, Jackie Burke, Gus Moreland, Harry Todd—all Texans.

There was also a vast amateur circuit you could travel, if you wanted to take your game out of town. All summer long, you could go play in invitation tournaments in towns like Ranger, Midland, Abilene, Wichita Falls, Waxahachie, Longview, Corpus Christi, everywhere.

In these tournaments, you would win shotguns, radios, silverware, lawn tools, and quite a bit of money in calcutta pools.

It was this amateur circuit that gave us Hogan, Nelson, and Demaret from the old days, and then Jackie Burke, Jr., Tommy Bolt, Billy Maxwell, Don Cherry, Don January, Earl Stewart, Dave Marr, Bill Rogers, Charlie Coody, Bobby Nichols, Miller Barber, Howie

Johnson, Ernie Vossler, Homero Blancas, Fred Marti, Jacky Cupit, and then in later years your Ben Crenshaws, Tom Kites, and John Mahaffeys.

Ernie Vossler, who got richer than A-rabs in Palm Springs, came right out of our game at the Hills.

Even then, he was a relentless competitor who never understood why anybody but him ever made a putt.

Sometimes, when Weldon the Oath, a postman, made a putt, Ernie would walk off the course, fuming.

Ernie was never as proficient as myself or John the Band-Aid at breaking clubs. I once broke the shaft on my 8-iron nine days in a row at the seventeenth because I couldn't make the ball hold that green, a par 3. But Ernie had his moments. He bladed a 6-iron one day in the sixth fairway and almost killed everybody. He hurled the club into the brick fairway, and the shaft snapped, and both parts of the club went into the air, and one jagged end sprang back and hit Ernie in the palm, causing five stitches, and another jagged end caught me in the leg. As the shafts sparkled in the sun, it was as if we were being attacked by lightning bolts.

And this was the man who knew nothing of golf before I had once recruited him for the golf team at Paschal High. He went on to win the Fort Worth city championship, which was something that Hogan, Nelson, and I could never do—we all finished second in our best effort—and Ernie won the State Amateur, and then some tournaments on the PGA Tour, and then he got into real estate and bought Oklahoma City and Palm Springs. Ernie Vossler became our honor graduate

But our most intriguing graduate was Weldon the Oath.

Weldon had talking fits—talking to the ball.

He would take oaths. He would rush out to the game so quickly, he would play golf in his postman's cap and without golf shoes, which could have had something to do with his chronic slice.

"All right, this is your last chance," Weldon would say to the ball as he waggled his driver. "You lousy little crud, if you slice on me one more time I'm gonna bite you in half and chew your rubber guts up. You're goin' straight this time, you hear me? You *hear* me tellin' you this? All right, then. Geeeeooood, daaaammmmmm, aaaaiii, ga!"

And Weldon would hit another slice.

It would cross two fairways to his right, a marvelous half-moon of a shot.

The ball would scarcely leave the club face before Weldon would start to spin around in circles, pawing at the air, slugging at imaginary evils. Frequently, he would dash over to the tee marker and start beating the driver on it. He would stomp on the club.

Then just as quickly, he would calm down and say, "Let me hit one more, I got to figure out what I'm doin' wrong."

And he would slice again.

That's when he would break the shaft over his knee. "Geeeeaaa, rrreeeeeaaa, aaaddd," he would snarl. "This is my last time on a golf course, you can book it! Gaaddd raaaap son of a baddered bat rop ditch bastard." When Weldon was hot, the words didn't come out right. "You picks have guyed me damn stick—this rotten, stinking, miserable, low-life spicky dop whore bubbin' game— feck it, babber sam!"

Weldon would hike to the clubhouse, but of course he would be back the next day.

It was in the last couple of years at Goat Hills, shortly

before the city sold those 106 acres to TCU so the school could build more cream-brick buildings, that the games grew too big, too expensive, for working men and college students.

Some of the guys got to where they couldn't pay when they lost, and others didn't want to collect it, and some of us were developing other interests—snooker, eight-ball, newspapers, divorces.

Moron Tom had something to do with the games disappearing, going the way of other endangered species.

He was a muscular, likable West Texan who had come to Fort Worth on a football scholarship at TCU, but had quit football when he found out you had to work out every day in the fall. He hit a long ball and he loved to bet, on anything. He could hold his breath longer than anybody, for money, or inhale a can of beer in four seconds, for money, and he rarely spoke English.

Everything was quadruple unreal to Moron Tom, or "Hit it fine, pork-e-pine," and many of the words he uttered were something else spelled backward.

"Cod Ee-rack Fockle-dim," for instance, was Dr. Cary Middlecoff spelled backward.

The day of one of the last big games, Moron Tom walked onto the porch and said, "I'll take toops and threeps from Youngfut, Youngjun, and Youngdump."

This meant Moron Tom wanted two up and three up from young Foot, young John, and young me.

"Ten and ten with Grease's men," he added, "and two and two with Joe-Magoo."

Everyone drifted out to the first tee.

Wagers were made, partners chosen, practice swings taken.

Moron Tom brought a big hook in from over the apartment houses and found the fairway.

"Think I can't, Cary Grant?" he said.

Magoo and I wound up as partners against all other combinations, and this was not altogether good—neither of us knew how to play safe, and Magoo was also unlucky. Once in the Glen Garden Invitation in Fort Worth—that's the course where Hogan and Nelson caddied as kids—Magoo hit a 285-yard tee shot but found his ball in a man's mouth, being cleaned.

We were in good form today, however. Teamed well for a blaze of birdies and had everybody bleeding to death by the time we got to the eighteenth.

I would hit a good drive and Moron Tom would say, "Cod Ee-rack Fockle-dim," and Magoo would hit a good drive, and Moron Tom would say, "Wod Daw-ret-sniff," meaning Dow Finsterwald spelled backward.

When either of us holed a putt, Moron Tom would say, "Take a nap, Einra Remlap," which was Arnie Palmer spelled backward.

By the time we came off the seventeenth green, Magoo and I had somehow birdied six holes in a row, and we calculated that if we only parred the eighteenth, we would win so much money we wouldn't be able to haul it home in Cecil's cookie truck.

Everybody pressed to get even, of course, on the eighteenth tee.

John the Band-Aid summed it up for most of the players, who must have numbered twelve in all, when he said, "I'm out, out, out, out, out, and out, and one down, one down, one down, one down, one down, and even. Want me to bend over?"

The eighteenth at Goat Hills was slightly uphill. You drove from a windy knoll with the south wind usually helping and aimed across a tiny creek and a couple of sycamore trees. A big drive would leave you only 30 or

40 yards short of the green, a flip and a putt from a birdie or a flip and two putts from an easy par.

Not to birdie the eighteenth often resulted in a wedge being broken, and not to par the eighteenth was unthinkable.

The only conceivable trouble was far, far to the right, across the tenth fairway, where Stadium Drive was out-of-bounds. But nobody had ever sliced that badly, not even Weldon the Oath, until Magoo did.

At the height of Magoo's backswing, when he was coming out of his shoes to try to drive the green and make us richer, Moron Tom quietly said, "Tissim, Oogam." Which was Miss it, Magoo" backward.

Needles were commonplace in the game. Coughing, sneezing, dropping a full bag of clubs, yelling, burping, all such things could be heard on backswings at times— you took it for granted and dealt with it.

But Magoo came apart with laughter at Moron Tom's remark and almost fell down like Cecil when he swung at the ball.

Even Magoo had to laugh again when Moron Tom said, "Oogam dewolb the Nepo," which translated into "Magoo blowed the Open."

To say this put extra pressure on me, with Magoo out of the hole, would be to say that the meat loaf in the lunchroom at Goat Hills contained grease.

Right here, I should explain that on the other side of the creek at the eighteenth, set upright into an embankment, was a storm drain about three feet in circumference. We often pitched at it with old balls from the ladies' tee, but it was a remarkable thing if anybody ever got one in there.

And from up on the men's tee, 100 yards or so back, it was an incredibly small target. In fact, I didn't even think about it as I got set to drive the green and make another birdie, or know the reason why. All I wanted to know was what everybody wanted engraved on their tombstones.

But at the top of my swing, Moron Tom whispered something else.

"Clutch, Mother Zilch," he said.

The club head hit about two inches behind the ball, and the drive snap-hooked into the ground just in front of the ladies' tee, took a big hop to the right off of some rocks, and—I swear to you—went straight into the storm drain.

It remains the only hole in one I ever made, and it was, you might say, the shot which semi-retired me from golf forever.

A Semi-Tough
Return to Golf

IT IS NO BIG SECRET that the game of golf requires grave concentration to be played decently, so let me say right off that it is not altogether to your advantage while you're standing over a 5-iron shot to be thinking, "I've got to remember to get some Freon in the Toyota."

Freon shots are my life these days. They are the kind of shots which, after you hit four inches behind them, float lazily into a lagoon or marsh. Freon shots are what happen to you all too often when you take up the game again after a ten-year layoff.

I call them Freon shots but they have other names, such as:

1. The Phillips screwdriver shot, as in "I know there used to be one in the kitchen drawer."

2. The frozen dinner shot, as in "I'm sure we're out of creamed chipped beef and chicken pot pies."

3. The electrician shot, as in "It's usually the circuit breaker, but this time it's not."

4. The VCR shot, as in "You would think the manual would tell you how to set the stupid timer."

And most familiarly:

5. The no-account, low-life, rotten summitch.

Actually, Freon shots come later. When you take up the game again after a long layoff, there is a more urgent problem.

The first thing you discover is that a golf club weighs in the neighborhood of 180 pounds and feels like you're trying to swing a parking meter.

A golf club didn't use to weigh this much. Not during all those years when I played at scratch around Fort Worth and won some tin against a pillaging bunch of barbers, filling station attendants, insurance salesmen, and deliverymen.

A golf club weighed next to nothing and the only thing I ever thought about it was that it better not betray me on a crucial shot in a heavy-duty gambling game unless it wanted to get drowned or have its neck broken on the trunk of a pecan tree.

Also, the golf club listened when I spoke to it.

It would perk up its little MacGregor head and pay attention when I would say something like "I'll tell you one thing. Slick Grip. Show me that banana ball again and I'll stuff your ass inside the trunk of that car over there and we'll see how you like it when you suffocate!"

The golf club would go quietly into the white canvas bag and vow never to hook again.

Nowadays, however, my Hogan Apex 9-iron, for instance, just sits there and glistens in the Florida sunlight while its shaft gets mysteriously longer and the club head gets mysteriously heavier—it can't wait for me to hit a cold shank or plow up a square foot of Bermuda on a simple pitch shot.

Once I even heard it call me a name off a Chinese

menu. That was after it made me hit a foot behind the ball from only 100 yards out and never even finish the easiest par 4 in North America after my best tee ball of the round.

"LOIBIP," is what it called me, as in Loss Of Interest, Ball In Pocket.

I think that's what it means, although it could mean minced pork in lettuce.

If I had hit a shot like that in the old days, I would have taken that whole bag of clubs and thrown them to the reptiles, and played out of somebody else's bag, and pressed everybody to get even, and tried to prove how much money I could lose in a single afternoon.

But when I commit such an atrocity today, inasmuch as score no longer matters, I just shrug and casually climb in the golf cart and smile at someone, and say, "Part of the charm."

Of course, there's another reason why you can't dump a whole bag of clubs into a haunting lagoon or river. That's because golf clubs today cost $4,768 apiece, and a full set of clubs that are perfectly suited to your swing takes 112 months for delivery.

The reason it takes so long to get them is because the director of golf at your country club, who used to be known as the club pro and only had one assistant instead of eight, is on the staff of the manufacturer.

As a golf writer, I had never stopped being *around* the sport, but the reason I started playing again is because I moved to Ponte Vedra Beach, Florida, after living in New York City for twenty-six years, and if you don't take up golf in Florida, there's not much else to do except become a real estate salesman.

Growing up in Fort Worth, the town that gave you Ben Hogan, Byron Nelson, and my once-fabled hook, I had played golf almost every day in my life for about twenty years, from the age of eight to the age of twenty-eight. I had kept on trying to play once or twice a month for the first twelve years or so that I lived in Manhattan, which wasn't easy. If you live in Manhattan, a round of golf in Westchester County, or out on Long Island, or up in Connecticut, or over in New Jersey, takes two days, counting travel time, and a year off your life, counting the aggravation.

But up until the late 1970s, possessing what some would call a natural swing, I could still go out and break 80 on any course you wanted to drop me on, and I could do it from the blues, which used to be known as the tips before some dirt salesman invented the gold tees, the platinum tees, the uranium tees, the Tiffany tees, and finally, at long last, four condos later, the championship tees.

Muscle memory would help me accomplish this. That and the fact that I was tournament-tough from all those earlier years of competing in high school and college and on the Texas amateur circuit against such legends such as Morris Williams, Jr., Billy Maxwell, Don January, Joe Conrad, Don Cherry, Earl Stewart, Ernie Vossler, and on and on; guys who could waltz me around the dance floor like I was some kind of Ginger Rogers.

Not that I didn't have my moments of glory as a Respectable Golfer.

In 1955 I was a serious contender for the Fort Worth City Championship, which at the time was thought by some of us to be second in prestige only to the U.S. Open. That summer, the tournament was contested over 72 holes of stroke play at Rockwood Muni, which was sort of a combination wind machine and watermelon field. There was one clump of trees on the whole course and they were all surrounding one green on the back nine. How they got there was as big a mystery as what a leopard was doing at that altitude on Kilimanjaro.

I stayed within a stroke or two of the lead all the way and then a demon inhabited my body and I birdied four of the last five holes of the final round to take on all the appearances of a sure winner. But while I sat on the clubhouse porch and rehearsed my victory speech, I finished second to a college player from North Texas State in Denton. He had taken the precaution of eagling one of the holes I had birdied, and that was the difference. He had also taken the precaution of moving to town about a day before the tournament started.

"Nice going, Harold," I said. "Spending a lot of time in the city these days?"

I was left to amuse myself with the thought that I had something else in common with Ben Hogan and Byron Nelson. They never won the City either.

All through the 1950s, I would play the occasional round with Hogan out at the Colonial Country Club, being known to Ben as someone who covered his deeds for the Fort Worth *Press.* Having a sense of history, I realized even then what an incredible privilege this was.

"Who did you used to play golf with, Daddy?"

"Oh . . . Ben Hogan."

I would wander out to Colonial and find Ben practicing somewhere, hitting knocked-down 3-irons he might need at Oakland Hills or Oakmont or Olympic. I would say, "What the hell is *that*?" He would say he needed it at Oakland Hills.

Once in a while he would say, "Let's go," and we would play 18, whereupon he would shoot what I thought was a flawless 66, though never holing a putt, and I would shoot a scrambling 76, though never missing a putt.

Ben squinted at my putter a lot, I remember. Now and again, he would take the Armour from me and look at it curiously and practice a few strokes with it but eventually hand it back and walk away toward the next tee, shaking his head with an expression I sensed to be a combination of disgust and disbelief.

One afternoon I got a critical tip from him.

On a par 4 at Colonial with only 125 yards to the pin and a stiff south breeze behind us, I watched him take out a 7-iron of all things and bounce it up for a gimme birdie.

"What in God's name was *that*?" I asked.

"You always overclub downwind," he explained.

Swell. I've been overclubbing downwind ever since, and it would be impossible to total up the number of balls I've hit over greens and into bunkers, rivers, orchards, backyard cookouts, and city streets.

In the spring of 1956, Ben invited me to join him and two other players out at Colonial in an 18-hole exhibition for the benefit of the United States Olympic Fund. This was the Olympics where we were going to send Bobby Morrow of Abilene, Texas, over to Melbourne, Australia, to whip up on the foreigners in the sprints, and Ben wanted to help out.

The other members of the foursome were Royal Hogan, Ben's brother, a former City champion, and Raymond Gafford, the pro at Fort Worth's Ridglea Country Club, a bettor's haven back then and something of a historic landmark in that it used to be one of Titanic Thompson's hangouts.

Raymond was a very stylish player, a guy who could

have made it on the PGA Tour if he had wanted to take a cut in pay from burying everybody in the high-rent gambling games at Ridglea.

I could only assume I was invited to be a part of the exhibition because in those days I was writing a daily column with my picture in it. Actually, it was the picture of a person I had never seen before in my whole life.

Owing to some idiotic delay at the newspaper office—no doubt a discussion with the editor in chief about my expenses on an excessively cosmopolitan business trip I'd taken to Wichita Falls—I arrived at the first tee just in time for the game.

I didn't really expect to find 3,000 people lining the first fairway, but I would deal with that later. I ripped off my coat and tie and rolled up the sleeves on my light blue buttoned-down shirt, teed up a ball, and waggled a driver.

No glove and no golf shoes yet.

"Wait a minute," said Hogan, staring at my ball. It was an old Spalding Dot that was turning the color of pewter. Ben came over and handed me two boxes of new balls.

"And put on your shoes before you hurt somebody," he said.

I got off the first tee without injury to anyone, but for the first four holes, with a severed case of gallery nerves, I either cold-topped or dart-hooked everything.

My swing must have looked as jerky as Charlie Chaplin in a silent movie, because, as we were walking down the fifth fairway, Ben said, "You could probably take it back faster if you tried."

I got the point.

I settled down and somehow managed to get around in 77 while Ben shot what I thought was the best round of recreational golf, tee to green, I had ever seen, a three-under 67. He hit every fairway and every green in regulation and the longest putt he made was a tap-in.

By the way, in those years Colonial was an unspeakably hard golf course. The fairways were brutally narrow, the rough was deep and uncultivated, and the Trinity River came more fiercely into play. The bent greens, first in the southwestern part of the United States (circa 1936), not only seemed to be the size of throwrugs, there were diabolical levels to them and they were guarded by huge oaks that have since died.

"What a great round," I said to Ben of his 67 later that day in the grillroom.

"That wasn't a good round of golf," he said, and his look told me he was serious.

I tried not to appear astonished.

He said, "A good round of golf is if you can hit about three shots that turn out exactly as you planned them, I didn't have any of those today."

I grinned. "Well, I wish I could miss every shot and shoot sixty-seven."

"It's possible," said Ben. "That's what's wrong with tournaments."

Hogan witnessed the best shot I ever hit in competition, but let me set it up properly.

It was a few years earlier, in 1950, my sophomore year at Texas Christian University, a thrilling time in the annals of Horned Frog golf, for I was the team's No. 1 player.

Somehow that spring, our team won enough matches and tied enough matches against Bears, Owls,

Aggies, Mustangs, and Razorbacks that we came down to the final match against the University of Texas at Colonial with the Southwest Conference championship on the line.

I, of course, knew the championship wasn't on the line. There was no living way we could beat Texas— Texas had Morris William, Jr.!

The son of an Austin sportswriter, Morris was a slender, wiry, supple, good-looking guy who never hit a crooked drive, never struck an iron that didn't sound pure and wasn't clotheslined to the flag, and never missed a putt he needed to make. He had a quick smile and a friendly nature, but on the golf course there was an ax murderer struggling to climb out of his heart. He had a beautiful upright swing and played along in the quick-hitting style of a Lanny Wadkins or Tom Watson. He had become a friend, through the Texas amateur circuit, but I was in helpless awe of his talent.

Morris William, Jr., was invincible, unbeatable, incomparable, and otherwise stupendous—the Ben Crenshaw of his day.

That I knew of, the only match he had ever lost was to North Carolina's Harvie Ward, one down in the 36-hole final of the 1949 NCAA championship, which was no great embarrassment if you knew anything about Harvie Ward.

This was during a more romantic time in our history when prominent members of TCU's varsity football team would come out to Colonial to caddie for us in college matches. School spirit deal, they said. It was a flattering thing, though very few of the gridiron heroes knew anything about golf.

The caddie for my match against Morris Williams,

Jr., that day was a burly, maniacal defensive end from Odessa named Billy Moorman.

As we were all fooling around on the putting green before the matches started, Billy quietly said to me, "We're gonna mop up on them teasippers today."

"Speak for yourself," I said.

"Naw, really," he said. "Look how skinny they are."

I figured there were two things that might help keep me from being totally humiliated by Morris. One, he had never played Colonial before, and two, Ben Hogan would be following us in a golf cart. Ben had read about this celebrated kid from Austin and wanted to take a look at him.

We played the back nine first to avoid a collision with some of Colonial's grumpiest members, and through fifteen holes, rather miraculously, I was all square with Morris and we were both even par. Quite frankly, I was playing my career round. I might even have been one up or two up if God had been wearing the purple of TCU instead of the orange of Texas.

But now we were at Colonial's par-4 seventh hole— our sixteenth—which back then called for a 1-iron or 4-wood off the tea and a 6-, 7-, or 8-iron to the green unless you wanted to try to thread a needle with the driver, in which case you'd have a pitching wedge to the green, the green being one of those shadowy throw rugs sheltered by tall, overhanging trees.

Smart money usually played it safe, but I was never known for that. So I sky-sliced a driver into the right rough behind a tall cluster of oaks.

I looked over at Hogan, who was sitting in the golf cart with Marvin Leonard, his old friend and the man who built Colonial. I put my hand to my throat and smiled weakly. Ben shook his head sadly. Meanwhile, Morris nailed it down the gut with a 4-wood.

I had a remote chance to reach the green on my second shot if I could get a 6-iron out of the Bermuda rough and up quickly over the trees and then down quickly over some more trees, which, curiously, is what happened. Don't ask me to write an instruction article on it. All I did was swing the club, and mostly out of anger at my tee shot. The ball barely cleared the trees going up, and barely cleared a front bunker coming down, and bit into the green and stopped about six inches from the cup.

"Gosh, Dan, great shot," said Morris from out in the fairway.

I said thanks and tried to act like the shot was merely a part of my normal repertoire.

The defensive end, my caddie, said, "There you go, son—nothin' two more of those won't cure."

I looked at him incredulously.

For the next long moment, while I waited for my opponent to spray his own approach out of shell shock, I entertained some wonderful thoughts. I had a gimme birdie, thus I was going to be one up on Morris Williams, Jr., with only two holes to play. I was going to *beat* Morris Williams, Jr. I was going to win the individual championship in the conference tournament next month. I was going to turn pro, go on the tour, wear beltless slacks, and complain about courtesy car drivers the rest of my life. I was . . .

This is about the time that Morris holed out his 7-iron for an eagle 2.

Yeah. Holed it out. Hit a 7-iron in there about 10 feet short of the flag. The ball took a gash out of the lush bent grass and rolled slowly past my 6-inch birdie and died in the cup—a deuce.

All I could do was laugh. All Morris could do was laugh, though apologetically.

Still laughing, I looked over at Ben Hogan. He was shaking his head again as he turned the cart around and headed for the clubhouse. I guess he knew the match was over.

Needless to say, it was. We both parred the last two holes, so with the lowest round I ever had on old Colonial, a one-under-par 69 from the tips, I lost one up, didn't win the conference the next month, never won the conference, didn't turn pro, and only went out on the tour with a typewriter.

(Although I'm not generally fond of parenthetical information, it would be incorrect for me not to mention here that Morris Williams, Jr., one of the nicest guys I ever knew and one of the best golfers I ever saw, was tragically killed in the crash of an Air Force jet in 1953. He had planned to go on the PGA Tour when he got out of the service. I don't have any doubt that he would have been a big star out there and would have given Arnold Palmer a run for his charisma.)

So much for the glory moments. I have relived a few of them only to acquaint you more intimately with the man who gave up the game completely for ten years.

I can't blame my loss of interest entirely on living in Manhattan. I think it had more to do with the time I went up to Winged Foot and discovered that virtually overnight, I could no longer get my swing around my stomach.

What had once been a reasonably controlled hook off the tee that would go 250 yards or so had suddenly turned into a pitiful slice of, oh, 174 yards.

Moreover, I had gone from a deft chipper and putter to a person more interested in idle gardening. And all of the clubs between the driver and putter were achieving the results of rakes and shovels.

I couldn't break 95. Thus, having once played well enough to tell tales and collect a cupboard of trophies my kids could throw away someday, it was not fun at all to play disgusting, rancid golf.

So I quit.

You may ask what I did for recreation for those ten years. Well, to start with, golf was never recreation for me. Golf was never anything but vicious competition and cerebral gambling—learning how not to get out-bet. I played a little family tennis, only because I discovered you can smoke at the net in family tennis. Largely, I drank a lot, traveled a lot, and worked.

It seems clear now that the most pleasure I got out of quitting golf was turnng down some invitations to play in the Crosby, as many of us still refer to it. It was most satisfying to turn down the Crosby, knowing there were so may CEOs who would sell their daughters to get invited.

I fondly treasure the many happy years of covering the Crosby and lifting beverages in Club XIX of the Pebble Beach Lodge for a week, secure in the knowledge that I didn't have to get up at 6 A.M. and wade through the ice plant.

As my friend Steve Reid, the ex-touring pro turned TV producer, once said, "There's nothing more boring than a golf tournament in the daytime."

Almost everything looks different when you reenter golf after a long layoff.

Take the clubs. In just about any golf shop I've entered, I've been able to find nothing but long rows of things that look like parts that have fallen off a DC-10.

I inquired and found out that these things are called metal woods.

They are, to me, as unsightly as the long rows of unfinished irons in the golf shops. I know they're unfinished because all of their backs are missing. You could pour a cup of soup in them or use them for a soap dish. Cavity backs, huh?

I happen to be a traditionalist. I play with a set of Hogan Apex irons, which look like irons and don't have the backs missing, and an old Tommy Armour putter—I don't want my putter to sound like a door chime or look like a power tool.

I *do* carry a 5-wood and a 7-silly, or what is more accurately known as a 7-wood. These clubs are the best of the modern inventions, especially the 7-silly, which eliminates the 1-iron, 2-iron, and 3-iron from your bag forever.

Off the pro tour, nobody has ever been able to hit a long iron with consistency or confidence. The only way to attempt it is with a debonair casualness while humming a medley of Broadway tunes.

People say my resentment of the new technology costs me three shots a nine these days, but since I only keep score on rare occasions, what difference does it make?

Peculiar questions are now asked of me in golf shops.

When I went up to the counter to buy my first dozen Titleists in ten years—Titleist being the only golf ball I remembered with fondness—a young assistant pro said. "Surlyn or balata?"

"My name's Jenkins," I said. "I'm playing with Mr. Herring at one-fifteen."

We straightened out that confusion and then the assistant pro said, "Do you want nineties or hundreds?"

"I suppose I'd rather shoot in the nineties," I said intelligently.

On another day at another club, I asked another young assistant pro if he had a set of leather head covers for sale.

He looked at me oddly and said, "Leather . . . ?"

Apparently, if you want a set of leather head covers today, you have to buy a calf, kill it, send it off to Dornoch in the north of Scotland, and wait two years for the owner of a primitive arts and handicrafts shop to sew it together.

In the meantime, you can buy a set of furry-fuzzy head covers in pink, red, green, blue, and yellow. This way your golf bag looks like dueling drum majors.

I understand how fortunate I am to live where I do, which is on Florida's "First Coast," halfway between Jacksonville and St. Augustine. My reentry to golf wouldn't have been possible otherwise. I'm only a matter of minutes from the first tee at Marsh Landing, Ponte Vedra, Sawgrass, or the TPC, four elegant clubs offering a total of 117 fascinating holes of golf, clubs I've been able to join for only a third of what it would cost to join Colonial back in Fort Worth, which still didn't have an ocean the last time I checked but did have a waiting list for both memberships and starting times.

In the beginning, my comeback was a festival of shanks and tops, plinks and pop-ups, scoops and scuffers. Agony. Torture. Nonsense.

I would play the front nine in 6, Pocket, Pocket, 5, Pocket, 6, Pocket, Pocket, Pocket.

"What did you shoot on the front?"

"Seventeen."

I would then play the back in 6, Pocket, 5, 6, 6, Pocket, Pocket, 6, Pocket.

No card.

For the first time in my life, I was forced to seek advice about hitting a golf ball. "Slow it down" was easier said than done. "Hold on less tightly" was next to impossible. "Get back on your heels" was helpful if I wanted to hit another foot behind it.

Roger Maltbie, one of the tour's venerable cigarette smokers and therefore someone I like, was the first person who told me something useful. When we happened to be in the same tavern one evening, I said, "Roger, in one sentence, cure my shank."

He thought about it a few seconds, and said, "Try to hit it left."

It worked. I no longer shank, but now I have to ask him another urgent question: How do I keep from hitting it left so often?

Early on in the agonizing, torturous, nonsensical days of my comeback, golf tried to kill me.

On the south nine at Sawgrass in late spring I was hacking around with a couple of friends one day and we came to the sixth hole, a par 5 that requires a drive, a lay-up, and a pitch over a lagoon. The lagoon is supported near the green by a bulkhead to keep the alligators from gnawing on the flagstick, or golf carts, and to keep the water moccasins from swallowing the Surlyns and balatas, or pecking at your ankles.

My pitch shot, a sickly thing, came down in the grass between the green and the bulkhead, and then my chip left enough to be desired that I spoke to it in Swahili, backed up, and smoldered.

But not for long. What I had forgotten is that the bulkhead and lagoon were directly behind me. Suddenly, I was standing on top of the bulkhead, losing my balance, flapping my arms like a demented person trying to fly, gaping over my shoulder at the lagoon, my eyes ablaze, knowing what horrors existed in the watery deep.

"Geeeaaad damn, aaaiiigh," is close to what I was saying before the splash, five feet down and into the mud and dark water, as two things raced through my brain. Alligators kill you—they drown you first, then chew you up. If that wasn't my fate, I was probably going to reenact the "river scene" from *Lonesome Dove.*

Fortuitously, the gators and moccasins were all preoccupied with other interests while I waded around, waist deep, in the lagoon, and I guess I don't have to tell you that I may have set a new gym, school, and conference record for the Terror-Stricken Sportswriter's Bulkhead Climb.

Splattered with mud and lagoon-drenched, I finished the round in the grand style of LOIBIP.

Since that day, I've slowly discovered that it's possible to enjoy golf, but only if you follow certain rules.

a. Play from the white tees only. Any 12-handicapper, square-groove, metal-wood, hot-ball, macho nitwit who wants to drag you back from the whites, shoot him.

b. Roll it over everywhere and don't swing at it until you have it sitting up perfectly. Airborne balls are most encouraging.

c. Keep in mind that you or others in your foursome can't make worse than a double bogey on any hole. Speeds up play.

d. Never look for lost balls more than five seconds. Drop one without penalty.

e. Hit till you're happy off the first tee, or any other tee if it suits your mood.

f. Don't try to blast out of bunkers. Either putt it out or take a free drop. Why risk blindness?

g. Tell the club manager you want to see the girl in the beverage cart every six holes.

h. Mulligans are free. Use them without guilt or embarrassment.

i. There is only one thing to say after hitting a shot into the water. "Surf's up, dude."

j. Never keep score unless by some weird coincidence you have a chance to break 80, 85, or 90 for the first time. Not keeping score eliminates much of the game's frustrations. On the other hand, if you come within a stroke of breaking 80, 85, or 90 for the first time, by all means count the practice shot you hit from the twelfth fairway, the one that went on the green. It was, after all, the shot you would have hit if you hadn't been thinking about Freon.

Even by the above rules, it took me a long four months of playing two and three times a week to get it down to where I could reasonably expect something decent to happen. Not long ago, I finally broke 80 at Marsh Landing.

Nobody wants to hear about anybody else's round, of course. I certainly don't. Start to tell me about your round of golf and I bolt for the door. Or my eyes glaze over and I topple out of my chair. I wouldn't think of doing this to anyone. But the first hole at Marsh Landing is this sporty little par 4 with big trouble on the right, so I cut my drive down the left side of the fairway, and . . .

Golf with the Boss

(Author's note: *A slightly longer version of this piece appeared originally in the September 1990 issue of* Golf Digest. *I don't really think it had anything to do with the subject's failure to win reelection. I blame that, sadly enough, on the increasing number of Americans who want the federal government to pay their green fees for them.*)

IT BECAME CLEAR to me one day that Mr. George Bush of 1600 Pennsylvania Avenue, Washington, D.C., is the best thing that's happened to golf since Teddy Roosevelt ran up San Juan Hill with a mashie niblick in his fist; since Dwight Eisenhower whistled a spoon onto Omaha Beach, a tough par 4 over water; in fact, since Gerald Ford ate the all-weather grip on a putter, believing it to be a tamale.

Why is President Bush the best thing that's happened to golf lately? I'll tell you why.

One, he is the only President of the United States who has ever known my name. Two, he is the only President of the United States who ever confessed to reading my stuff. Three, he is the only President of the United States who ever invited me to play golf with him.

I should explain right here that the President and I became friends because he has immaculate taste in literature. On the bookshelves of his private office at Camp David, you will find the usual heavy stuff, such as *Semi-Panama Its Ownself* by Manuel Noriega, and *Dead Solid Broke* by Mikhail Gorbachev, but you will also find my complete works: *Farewell to Pars, The Old Man and the 7-Wood, Tender Is the Tee Shot, Moby Grooves,* and *The Score Also Rises.*

This is how we got to know one another. President Bush follows sports with a keen interest when he's not helping shove Communism into an unplayable lie. He enjoys watching sports on TV, talking sports, and reading about sports.

Thus, me being a sports guy, my wife and I found ourselves receiving invitations to a White House lawn party.

That day on the White House lawn, while a Navy combo in dress blues was playing good country music, while Millie, First Dog, was brought out to frolic, while horseshoes were pitched, and while a lot of deficit-worriers were hitting the food line, I had a few occasions to chat with the President on a variety of subjects, one of which was golf.

"How good a golfer are you, Mr. President?"

I had always thought that if I ever met a President of the United States, I would address him as "Mr. President" rather than "Yo, babe," the greeting often used by athletes who visit the White House.

That afternoon, the President said he had once been a tolerable golfer, years ago when he lived in Midland,

Texas, but that he wasn't too hot anymore, although he loved to "hack" at the game when he could find the time.

I said, "In your job, I guess it's better if you don't have a real low handicap."

He laughed. Not convulsively, but enough that I didn't get kicked out of the joint.

A little later on, the President said, "My problem with golf is I have to deal with a humiliation factor."

There were ways around that, I said. White tees only, roll it over everywhere, mulligans were free.

"Can't take a mulligan," he said. "Too much pride."

I said, "Mr. President, let me tell you something. I've been around the game a long time. Par doesn't give a damn about pride. I've seen par wring pride's neck."

We discussed the possibility of a golf game somewhere down the road.

A few weeks later, I received a self-typed note from him saying he had been working on his game a little and he was finally seeing the light at the end of the short-game tunnel. The short game had always been his biggest problem where golf was concerned. He mentioned he would arrange a game for us someday soon, if I was available.

"Have graphite shafts, will travel," I thought to myself.

President Bush, incidentally, is an inspiration to anybody who yearns to give up ice-cream sundaes. He's sixty-six but can pass for twenty years younger, a vigorous, athletic, flat-bellied man who not only likes golf, he likes baseball, football, plays tennis, dabbles in wallyball, pitches horseshoes with the best. He works out on cycles, Stairmasters, treadmills. Three times a week he jogs two miles, averaging about nine minutes a mile. He wishes his schedulers could find more time for him to go bonefishing and quail hunting.

You could take comfort that he's an inspiration in another way. Here is a man who has served his country in more different jobs than perhaps anybody in history—decorated Navy pilot of a torpedo plane in World War II, U.S. congressman, UN ambassador, ambassador to China, CIA director, Vice President, and now as the Boss. Try that on for a résumé.

I missed the first opportunity to play golf with him. He called me at home in Ponte Vedra Beach, Florida, to ask if I could come up to Washington, D.C., and complete a foursome with a couple of Democrats in the Senate. Two guys who were important to him in trying to get things done for the country, I assumed. He didn't name them. I had to beg off because I had just been released from the hospital after suffering what my wife said was a heart attack but what I knew was a fake heart attack brought on by the fast bent greens at Marsh Landing and the bunkers at Sawgrass, my home courses in Ponte Vedra. The President wished me a speedy recovery and said we would reschedule, but of course a good bit of time passed as such trifling things as summits and some guy in Iraq and the economy kept intruding on his golf.

Along in here, I received another self-typed note from him in which he acknowledged that the economy was batting about .187—his words—but he was hopeful of getting something done to improve it, and in which he observed that the guy in Iraq was a "bad dude," and something might have to be done about him, too, but eventually we *would* play golf.

Then one day I got another phone call, one that caused some merriment among friends. It came to the pressroom at Medinah in Chicago when Hale Irwin and Mike Donald were on the last few holes of their playoff for the U.S. Open.

I had been out on the course on the front nine of the playoff, but now I was watching it on TV in the press lounge with a couple of old comrades, Jim Murray of the Los Angeles *Times* and Blackie Sherrod of the Dallas *Morning News.* Somebody came up and told me I had a long-distance call at the front desk.

"*Now?*" I said incredulously. "In the middle of this?"

"Radio guy," Murray said.

"Yeah, probably," I said. "Some nitwit wants to know what I think of Cameroon going into the Southeastern Conference."

I refused to budge, except to go get coffee. But two minutes later, a Medinah press volunteer rushed up and said, "You may want to take the call. It's from the White House!"

Murray and Sherrod glanced at each other, and Blackie said, "He knew to look for you indoors."

I power-walked to the phone at the front desk.

"Dan, where did they find you?" a voice said.

"I'm in the pressroom at Medinah, Mr. President. I'm at the U.S. Open."

"Well, of course you are," said the President. "I'm watching it. Listen, I won't keep you, but I flew over this course the other day. It looks pretty interesting. Can you come up next Friday? We'll play eighteen, go to a minor-league baseball game, and spend the night at Camp David."

Want to talk about an offer you can't refuse?

Five days later I discovered myself milling around in the Oval Office with the Boss and the other two invitees who would complete our foursome: Walter Payton, the retired Chicago Bears running back who has settled into immortaldom, and Congressman Marty Russo, a severely low-handicap Democrat from Illinois.

The Oval Office looks like a neat place to go to work every day. Paintings, Western sculptures, windows on two sides through which you can see where Ike's putting green used to be, and some trees Andrew Jackson planted. The door stood open to the outer office, and there was laughter out there—a happy staff. The President showed us some objets d'art, gathered everybody around for a photograph, and said. "Let's go to lunch."

I knew we wouldn't be eating at a McDonald's, but I hadn't expected to go up to the dining room of the private residence of the White House. We walked down a hall, got on an elevator, and stepped off near the Lincoln Bedroom. The President then led us on a tour of the residence pointing out things of interest, with great pride and enjoyment. I was reminded of some American history I hadn't retained from Paschal High and Texas Christian University in Fort Worth.

We lunched on a light pasta, green salad, homemade peach ice cream. We made Gorbachev talk, S&L bailout talk, try-to-fix-the-economy talk, and golf talk.

Just after lunch, a pleasant-looking gentleman stepped off the private elevator, as if he had access to the President whenever he chose. I was delighted to learn that he does. It was General Brent Scowcroft, the National Security Adviser. He was accompanied by two other gentlemen.

"Excuse me, I better go talk to these guys," the President said. They all went into the living room and sat down.

I wandered back into the Lincoln bedroom and out onto the balcony to smoke and gazed out at the Washington Monument in the distance and down at Marine

One, the dark green chopper sitting on the White House lawn. I watched my golf bag being loaded.

The President's confab with the National Security Adviser only lasted a few minutes.

"No big deal?" I uttered inquisitively as were going down on the private elevator.

"No big deal," he said, smiling.

I couldn't help thinking back to a morning when I was on the set of the *Today* show with Tom Brokaw, who was then the host. Tom had been kind enough to have me on the show to plug a book that badly needed plugging. But during a commercial break, Brokaw took a call from a phone by his side.

Stunned, he turned to me and said, "Anwar Sadat's been shot."

So much for the book plug.

What's the point? Only that most writers are selfish, cynical, desperate swine who always expect the worst. I was relieved that the guy in Iraq, or another loon in another part of the world, hadn't done something that would cancel the golf game.

Down on the ground floor now, we were heading toward the door leading out to the chopper when the President said, "Wait a second. Let's go have some fun."

He walked past two guards and around a tall screen where a White House tour was in progress. Hordes of tourists were crammed into a corridor and up a staircase. Shocked and overwhelmed to see the President his ownself, when it was the last thing they had expected, they burst into whoops and applause.

He went over to shake hands, do high fives, exchange pleasantries. Returning to our group, he said, "Heck it's *their* house and *their* President. They deserve to see the guy."

I must tell you that Marine One is a nice way to travel. Forward in the cushiony, comfortable, remarkably quiet chopper were the President, the congressman, myself, Walter Payton, and Walter's nine-year-old son, Jarrett, who would have some tales to tell when he went back to school. Seated behind us were a handful of staff and Secret Service personnel, the earpiece and talk-box brigade.

There was no decor on Marine One except for the Presidential seal on the door to the flight deck and a small painting of the Boss's house in Maine. Out the window I think I might have noticed some other choppers flying escort.

We landed somewhere in the Maryland hills and got into a limo with the President. Then in a fifteen-vehicle motorcade that included a SWAT van, we rode through the countryside. When a President goes to play golf, it involves a bit more than donning the old cleats.

For security reasons, the Holly Hills Country Club in Ijamsville, Maryland, (the *j* is silent), had not been given much warning about "Guess who's coming to play golf today?" But word had quickly circulated to about two hundred members and friends, and when we got there they had already been frisked and told their dos and don'ts by the Secret Service.

The President shook a lot of hands and autographed a lot of golf caps and we all suited up in the locker room and hit a few practice balls and took a few putts. From Marlin Fitzwater, the White House press secretary, I had been informed that the pool of press photographers and writers would only be allowed to show up on the first tee, the ninth green, the tenth tee, and the eighteenth green. Otherwise we would have the course to ourselves.

Along with having your own jet, your own helicopter and your own song, I marked this as being one of the great perks of being President. No creepers and crawlers to play through on a golf course.

The owner of the Holly Hills Country Club, a lady named Ann Grimm, was on hand to greet us and answer some of my questions.

The club was fourteen years old. She had owned it for the past three, but was in the process of taking it equity. It had an upper-middle-class membership. The course had been designed by an architect named Robert Russell, who was said to be a "local fellow." The layout was generally ranked among the tenth best in the Mid-Atlantic PGA section.

"You're being discovered," I said.

"Isn't it wonderful?" she replied.

"Where am I?" I asked.

(Travel note: If I had been driving, I was a little under an hour from D.C. Take 270 west to 75 north to 144 and look for the Holly Hills Country Club sign, or the red-brick, two-story clubhouse.)

In the golf shop, the President swapped his Texas Rangers baseball cap for a Holly Hills cap, to go along with his red golf shirt, khaki slacks, and brown DryJoys.

On the first tee, the President slipped on an old white glove that was turning to rust. It looked like it had been worn by a tree planter a decade earlier.

"Hey, whoa," I said, getting a new Hogan glove out of my bag and handing it to him. "Don't embarass me."

"I never turn down a free glove," he said.

Glancing at the old one again, I said, "I guess you don't get many offers."

The Holly Hills course plays to 6,800 yards from the blues, par 72, but looking out on all the deep valleys and swollen hills to confront us, I suggested we play from the whites, a journey of about 6,500 yards. Nobody protested.

I also put the hit-till-you're-happy rule into effect for the cameras on the first tee. The President didn't actually approve of this until his first drive was a grounder, then he liked the idea.

He has a good swing. He's a natural left-hander who plays right-handed—like Ben Hogan, I told him. He doesn't take it all the way back to horizontal but he follows through nicely, and when he catches it on the screws, it goes. His mulligan was a beauty. People applauded.

In the lusty tradition of most sportswriters, I sky-hooked one about 215 yards. Walter Payton swung a little better than the usual ex-running back. With a long-iron, he smacked a towering slice that must have carried 300 yards. If he had hit the ball with one of his bulging forearms, it might have carried 500 yards. Marty Russo, the congressman, only had to take one stylish, powerful swing for me to see why he had been the congressional golf champion ten times.

Anyhow, we were away.

In our entourage of golf carts were Secret Service guys, a medical doctor, a White House photographer, an aide or two, and a fellow carrying a black briefcase, who would often be seen strolling along, by himself in the rough. A convivial Secret Service agent name Lou would never be more than a few feet from the President at all times. I gathered it would be Lou's job to hurl his body in front of the President in case I shanked a 5-iron.

Throughout the round I would take a club out of the bag and start to line up a shot, but would be distracted by the sight of a golf cart on a distant hilltop. Up there, two men would be peering through huge pairs of binoculars at—I don't know—Pennsylvania or something.

I looked through the binoculars once. I won't say they're powerful, but if I had been facing a window of the White House, seventy miles away, I could have read Abe's signature on the Emancipation Proclamation in the Lincoln Bedroom.

On the first three holes, the President encountered some trouble with his pitching and chipping, mainly because he was rushing his swing. He plays fast, I am happy to report, and likes to play fast, and doesn't understand why anybody would play slowly.

He could do mankind a wonderful service, I suggested, if he signed into law the death penalty for slow-playing golfers.

"I've never had a golf lesson," he confided.

"That's a natural swing—really?"

"Yep. For better or worse."

It was for the better. And it got him his first par on the 50-yard fourth hole, an up-and-over par 5 with a dogleg to the right. Good drive, good fairway wood, good pitch, two putts.

"Way to go, Boss," said the congressman, as the President holed a five-foot second putt for his par.

It was after the President had made a par that I felt at ease in nodding toward the man with the briefcase, and saying, "Is that what I think it is?"

"Yeah, the situation phone," he said.

I stared at the briefcase off and on for the rest of the day. The phone never rang. Knowing there's a situation phone around doesn't make golf any easier, if I may say so.

As a longtime captive of the game, I am a collector of

memorable stretches of golf holes. Things like Amen Corner at the Augusta National, the eleventh, twelfth, and thirteenth. Eight, nine and ten at Pebble Beach— Abalone Corner. The sixteenth, seventeenth, and eighteenth at TPC—Deane's Bad Dream, or whatever you want to call it.

To this list I would almost be tempted to add the sixth, seventh, and eighth at Holly Hills. Rugged, scenic, beguiling.

More or less ignorant of the dangers on these holes, I'm sure we got through them better than we would if we ever played them again.

The sixth, a 480-yard par 4, sharp dogleg left, might be the toughest hole in Western civilization, You have two choices off the tee box. Drive it straight and go out-of-bounds over a little fence, or hit a soaring hook up and over the tall trees and pray that the ball stays out of the forest. If you take a lesser club than a driver off the tee to stay in the narrow fairway, you can't get home.

Me and the Boss and Walter Payton ricocheted our way to bogeys at the sixth, and Marty Russo parred it only because he happened to sink a downhill, 20-foot putt over the slick bent-grass green.

The President hit his best shot of the day at the seventh. He nailed a 3-iron that cleared the water and bunkers and left him an 18-foot birdie putt. As destiny would have it, I hit one of my best shots of the day here, a 7-wood that stopped three feet behind the flag.

"You dog!" said the President. "What did you hit?"

"The trusty 7-wood," I said.

"A 7-wood? What's that?"

I said, "Some people say it's a 3-iron/4-iron, but I say it's the secret to a happy life."

As if to inspect the legality of it, the President fondled

my wooden, custom-made 7-wood, or 7-Silly, as it is known in some circles.

The ninth hole is a par 5 that goes back uphill to the clubhouse, where the cameras would be waiting. For the cameras, I half-bladed a 9-iron third shot and then three-putted for a disgusting bogey on what was an easy hole, but it was an eventful hole for the congressman. He rolled in a 25-footer for a birdie and had a momentary out-of-body experience.

Shouting and hopping around, he yelled, "Can you *believe* it? This is the greatest minute of my life! I'm with the *President* and *I birdie* the hole for CNN!"

Calmly, I said, "Marty, do you really want your constituents to know how well you play golf?"

Incidentally, if it's a fact that a man reveals his true character on a golf course, I can only attest that the President was easier to be around than any captain of industry I've ever been paired with in a pro-am. He seemed also to take himself far less seriously than any CEO of any plastics company I've ever encountered. He was the friendliest and most relaxed person in every room, and on every fairway.

He frequently walked to the green from 100 yards in, and bummed rides on everybody's golf cart. Thanks to my incessant questioning between shots, he spoke of many things other than golf—of food, of travel, of other sports, of Gorbachev's sense of humor. "He told me a lot of jokes when we weren't working," the President said. "And he asks more questions than you do—what does that car cost, what does a house like that cost?"

We all did ourselves proud for the cameras at the tenth tee. It was a downhill par 4 with plenty of room, and we could jump at our drivers. I thought I had seriously hurt my tee ball until the President made a good pass and fired it past me.

Down the steep hill, we found his ball five yards ahead of mine in the fairway. I didn't see how this had been possible, him with the funny Yonex and a Titleist and me with my secret weapons, a Mizuno and an Ultra.

"You killed that one, Boss," the congressman said. "I clock it at two-eighty."

"I don't know how," the President said.

"You made a good swing," I explained.

"Well, it comes and goes." He struggled. "If I can just get rid of the humiliation factor . . ."

The President made three pars on the back side and would have made two others if he hadn't three-putted. He played better as the day wore on.

The twelfth hole, a 145-yard par 3, is worth recalling. Here, the President, from about 130 yards away, hit a crisp 9-iron onto the green only 12 feet from the cup. He missed the birdie putt, which I attributed to his use of the long putter. This hole was also where a cluster of club members sneaked onto the course and were permitted to gallery the game and playfully holler at the participants. I assumed they had already been frisked by the Secret Service.

"How do you like the course, Mr. President?"

"Great!"

"How's your game?"

"Yeah."

Laughter.

Another laugh came when I hit a poor shot, a timid chip from the edge of the green that left me 10 feet short of the hole.

A wit in the gallery said, "Does your husband play golf too?"

Chuckling, the President said, "I hadn't heard that one."

By my scoring, the President shot a two-mulligan 86, "Sweetness" Payton shot a three-mulligan 85, I shot a three-mulligan 78, and Marty Russo shot a one-mulligan 68, four under par. A shocking display, I thought, for a public servant.

We showered and changed in the Holly Hills locker room and motorcaded to dinner at the Jug Bridge seafood restaurant in Frederick, Maryland, a tasty roadhouse the Secret Service had selected. After dinner, we motorcaded to Hagerstown, and to the elation of 3,500 people trooped into a Class AA baseball park to watch Hagerstown beat Harrisburg, 6–3. We sat just past the third-base line and the President waved and chatted with the faces of America, and admired the rich natural turf, and gazed at the old factory rising above the right-field wall, and smiled at the Moose Lodge sign out in center. "This is great," he said.

Americans tossed him baseballs to autograph and toss back. He made some good one-handed catches.

Close by, a fan got the Boss's attention, gave him a thumbs-up sign, and hollered, "I know what you're going through—I'm president of my city council back home!"

The President broke up laughing.

I sat there wondering when a President of the United States had ever been to a minor-league baseball game, or if one ever had. It pleased me that this was something the old Yale baseball captain had wanted to do.

On to Camp David, then, to spend the night. As resorts go, you take whatever you want in Palm Springs or Hawaii, and I'll take Camp David.

Run by the Navy, these lush and leafy 200 acres in the

Catoctin Mountains of Maryland have been special to every President since Franklin D. Roosevelt chose the property back in 1942 as a place where the Commander in Chief could go to relax, revitalize himself, and get some work done away from the microscope of the press and the often ceremonial Oval Office.

FDR originally called the retreat Shangri-la. It was Ike who changed the name to Camp David, for his grandson. Consisting of a number of rustic but comfortably furnished cabins scattered among the trees, of heavily shaded pathways, and of every conceivable type of recreational facility, the grounds are at your complete disposal once you're inside the compound as the Boss's guest.

In my cabin, I could have picked up the phone and asked an officer serving under Commander Mike Berry to send over any one of 300 movies in the film library for my VCR, or I could have lit a fire and explored all of the available beverages, or I could have gone for a midnight ride on all the bicycles outside my cabin door—and apparently without getting shot.

Instead, I fell to sleep in a large cozy bed that, having a sense of history, I hoped had been slept in by such high handicappers as Khrushchev, Brezhnev, Gorbachev, Maggie Thatcher, or Menachem Begin.

I was up early the next morning to throw the switch on the coffee machine and read the Washington *Post* and the New York *Times* that had been delivered to my cabin door. As suggested by the President the night before, I strolled down to have breakfast at Laurel Lodge, which is also where his office is located.

I was foolishly standing around among the umbrellas and tables on the veranda of Laurel, wondering where the entrance was, when a voice through a sliding-glass door summoned me to come in. The President, in a windbreaker, golf shirt, khakis, and Top-Siders, was alone in his office, pecking away on a typewriter. He said he had been at work since six-thirty.

His rather modest workplace at Camp David had more interesting memorabilia than most offices. There was a large painting of the torpedo plane he flew in World War II, and a model of it on his desk. In a tiny wooden box, which he was pleased to open, was a leather-band wristwatch Gorbachev had given him. Framed on a wall was a cardboard target with "Bush" scrawled on it and Noriega's bullet holes riddled in it— a souvenir brought back to him by the Panama invasion troops.

I left him to his work and went to have breakfast, but, as instructed, I returned to his office.

"Good grub," I said. "A guy could eat well in this job."

He grinned, stood up, and said, "Come on."

We got in his golf cart and he took me on a tour of the whole retreat, dropping little tidbits of lore along the way. He pointed out the beautiful little chapel he'd had built—each occupant apparently did something to improve Camp David.

I guess I was surprised to discover that Camp David had not had a church before now, but I didn't comment on it.

Presently, he stopped the golf cart in front of one of the older cabins. The sign on it said "Holly."

He said, "You might want to go sit on that bench there on the front porch for a minute."

I didn't ask why, I just did it, long enough to light a cigarette. When I got back in the cart, he smiled at me with a certain amount of relish, and said; "That's where

FDR and Churchill sat when they were planning the D-Day invasion."

"Jesus," I mumbled.

We cruised around a while longer and eventually he drove me down to a sedan parked at Aspen Cabin, the presidential residence, from where an Army sergeant would transport me to Washington National, about an hour away.

How could I thank him for the whole outing, other than to say I would vote for him five or six times in '92?

I did tell him to try to keep taking it back slowly.

As the car pulled away, I looked across a gorgeous lawn and my eyes lingered on the well-manicured bent-grass green of Ike's par-3 hole, which sits very near Aspen Cabin.

The pin was up front today. A 7-wood might be too much club.

"You'll Not Do That Here, Laddie"

IT WAS a gray, drizzly day like most others in Scotland and there was I, a lonely shepherd, strolling along a swollen dune by the North Sea looking for a wee stane to hit wi' a bit crook. Clumps of heather were up to my knees and the yellow-tipped whin was up to my chest, and I was up to here with my sheep because the little dumplings had wandered away. I had this crooked stick in my hand which I normally used to keep the dumplings in line. You know. Firm left side, eye on the tailbone, slow backswing—and whap. But they were gone and I was just ambling along when I saw this chuckie stane, as it was called, this round pebble. I also saw this rabbit scrape, as it was called, through an opening in the heather and whin. So I said to myself, "Self, why don't you take your bit crook and try to knock this here stane into that there scrape? And stay out of the heather because, boy, it'll make your hand ring." Well, I guess I took it back a little outside because I cut a low one right into the garbage and almost never did find it, but anyhow, this is how I came to invent the game of golf a few hundred years ago.

There are those, of course, who claim that I did not invent golf in another life, nor did any other Scot. Some say the Romans did it long before me and called it *Paganica,* which I think, between you and me, sounds like a joint over on East 56th. Some say the Dutch invented golf, or a game called *kolven,* which was similar. But no way. *Kolven* has to be a roll of veal stuffed with cheese and chives. Some say that even the French originated golf under the name of *jeu de mail,* but as any European traveler knows, this is a card game for the big players in Monaco. Actually, if the historians want to be picky, you could say that the Chinese a thousand years ago probably played a form of golf by batting a few snow peas around with chopsticks.

The fact of the matter is, golf is a Scottish game. It is naturally Scottish, as natural to our instincts as the seaside links land is natural to the setting. It was the Scots, after all, who took the game and did something with it when everybody else was busy making crossbows. We made the courses and the clubs, the balls and the rules, the trophies and the tournaments. We invented wind and rough, hooks and slices, bunkers and doglegs, and we were just getting ready to invent the overlapping grip when Harry Vardon, an Englishman, beat us to it.

We looked at the seashores, our links land, and said this is where the glory's at. Let the wet wind blow in from Denmark, or wherever it comes from. Let the incursions of the sea make the giant dunes and the tumbling valleys. Let the birds bring in the mixture of seeds that will grow our curious rough—the wiry, purple heather, the bulging whin, the dead fern we'll call bracken, and the green broom that does not have thorns to distinguish itself from the whin, or gorse. Let the rabbits and the foxes chew out the first fairways and dig the first cups, perhaps at St. Andrews where the Old Course lies today.

I don't know what the Romans, the Dutch, and the French were doing around the 1450s—aside from waiting for the Bible to get printed—but us Scots were playing golf then, and had been. At least we were when the kings would permit it, there being, from time to time, this nagging problem of national service. Had to go fight the English. Cancel my starting time.

There was this afternoon, I recall, when the game came close to being banished forever. As it happened, I was out on this moor at St. Andrews trying out a new Auchterlonie driving spoon at the eleventh—the short hole—when a King's guard raised up out of the whin and handed me a scroll signed by our monarch.

The scroll said, "It is decreetid and ordained that the Futeball and the Golfe be utterly cryit doune, and nocht to be usit."

"Guy never could spell," I said.

The guard pointed his crossbow at me and said that the King, Jimmy the Roman Numeral, meant business.

"The golfe is sik unprofitabill sportis," he said.

"Pal, you got that right," I said. "See that shepherd over there with the cross-handed grip on his bit crook? Well, he's got me out, out, out and one down."

"Don't be abusit," the guard said. "It is statute and ordinit that in na place of the realme be there Golfe in tyme cuming."

"Look," I said. "Smell that air. Gaze over this land. Great, huh? Who would want a guy to be hanging around a drafty castle waiting for an Englishman to scale the wall?"

"Aye," he said. "The aire is guid and the field reasonable feir. But can ya na handle the bow for archerie? Can ya na run or swoom or warstle instead?"

"I don't know, man," I said. "Let me put it your way. Here's the deal. I was drivin' the chuckie stanes wi' a bit stick as sune's I could walk."

He nodded his head as if he was beginning to understand.

"Here's something else," I said. "I happen to know that a bow maker in Perth is fixing up a set of clubs for the King right now. Why? Because the King sneaked out the other day to see what this game was all about and the Earl of Bothwell, who plays to a cool 23, brought him to his knees on the back three at Leith. The King's getting a pretty good price, too. Like only 14 s's for the set, whatever an s is."

The guard put down his crossbow and said, well go ahead and play if that was the case. And by the way, he added, did I want to buy "a dussen guid golfe ballis?"

"Hold it," I said. "You got featheries?"

"Aye," he said. "Guid featheries that cum from the Laird of Rosyth. Guid featheries stuffed with flock and wuid shavings."

"Four s's," I said. "And not an s more."

"Eight s's," he said.

"They're hot, man. Six s's and we both get out clean," I said.

He went for the six—you can always strike a bargain in Europe—and disappeared into the whin. And now that I had saved golf, I couldn't wait to try out one of the new high-compression featheries. I heeled up a good lie, and gave the shot a full body turn. Wow. Up, up, it soared—five yards, ten yards, twenty yards, and back to earth, whatever that was, only a short rake-in from the eleventh scrape, a par 12. There is still a hole in the wind where I hit that shot, and I thought to myself, what a happy and golden time, indeed.

In a few more years, all of royalty would be playing golfe. There were rumors of Mary Queen of Scots shanking all around the fields of Seton when some said she should have been mourning the demise of Lord Darnley. Charles the First got a very bad press for being in a match at Leith when the Irish Rebellion broke out. A lot of Jameses and Dukes of York were seen swinging at Musselburgh, which still claims to be the oldest layout in the world and now sits inside a race course near Edinburgh. There was a Stuart or two spotted in a putting game at Leith, which is where the Honourable Company of Edinburgh Golfers got started before they built Muirfield.

All golfers, I think, should be indebted to a small group of us that got together in 1744—the Honourable Company. Looking back, I don't know how we managed it without the Duchess of Argyll, but what we did was form the first country club. Not only that, we sat down and wrote the first rules of the game, which we called the Articles & Laws in Playing Golf. At the time, some felt our days might better have been spent defending Culloden against the English, but it just goes to show how important we thought golf was.

Those first rules have been well preserved along with some terribly clever comments I made at the meetings as I spoke keenly above the roar of our first president, Duncan Forbes. The thirteen rules of our first code are as follows:

1. You Must Tee your Ball within a Club length of the Hole.

(It's going to be uproarious fun, guys, waiting for somebody to drive before you can putt.)

2. Your Tee must be upon the Ground.

(Nothing like teeing up the ball in the air for greater distance.)

3. You are not to Change the Ball which you Strike off the Tee.

(The caddies will take care of this. When I tried to put down a clean one to putt the other day at St. Andrews, my man, Ginger Johnson, tugged at the sleeve of my cashmere and said, "You'll not do that here, laddie.")

4. You are not to Remove Stones, Bones, or any Break Club for the Sake of playing your Ball Except upon the fair Green and that only within a Club length of your Ball.

(Well, we'll get some pretty tricky breaks over the stones and bones.)

5. If your Ball come among Water, or any Watery filth, You are at Liberty to take out Your Ball, and throwing it behind the hazard 6 yards at least, You may play it with any Club, and allow your Adversary a Stroke, for so getting out your Ball.

(Unless your Adversary doesn't see you do it.)

6. If your Balls be found any where touching one another. You are to lift the first Ball, till You play the last.

(I estimate the odds on this happening at, roughly, 9,768 to 1.)

7. At holeing, You are to play your Ball honestly for the Hole, and not to play upon your Adversary's Ball, not lying in your way to the Hole.

(I heard about this across the ocean in a place called East Hampton. They call it croquet.)

8. If you should lose your Ball, by its being taken up, or any other way, You are to go back to the Spot where you Struck last, and drop another Ball, and Allow your Adversary a Stroke for the Misfortune.

(And if your Adversary has been seen taking up your Ball, you may strike your Adversary wi' a bit crook, teeing him upon the Ground.)

9. No Man at Holeing his Ball, is to be Allowed to Mark his way to the Hole with his Club or anything else.

(And if you do, man, the greens committee will wear your ass out.)

10. If a Ball be Stop'd by any person, Horse, Dog, or any thing else, the Ball so Stop'd Must be Played where it lyes.

(Yeah, but with big money up, how do you know if it's a real dog?)

11. If you draw your Club, in Order to Strike, and proceed so far in the Stroke as to be bringing down your Club; if then your Club shall break, in any way, it is to be accounted a Stroke.

(And your forearms will hum a merry tune as well.)

12. He, whose Ball lyes furthest from the Hole is Obliged to play first.

(This is a good rule, but I'll tell you, the public course players are going to relax it a little.)

13. Neither Trench, Ditch, or Dyke, made for the preservation of the Links, Nor the Scholars Holes or the Soldiers Lines, shall be Accounted a Hazard, But the Ball is to be taken out, Teed and played with any Iron Club.

(Oh, swell, Duncan. So how come you let me make eight passes at it yesterday in the Soldiers Lines with no relief?)

Well, you know what happens. You let one private club get started and down the road another pops up. The noblemen and lairds of Fifeshire couldn't stand it that we had the Honourable Company and some rules, especially, they said, when *everybody* knew St. Andrews was the cradle of golfe. So in hardly any time at all, they formed a group called the Society of St. Andrews Golfers, which later became known as the Royal & Ancient Golf Club. And you know what happened after that. They had the sport by the old gutta percha and never would turn loose of it.

A lot of arguments have gone on through the years about the history of the game, where it began, who molded the first cleek, and so forth. Over at Muirfield where the Honourable Company still hangs out, they say that the R&A would still be the Greensboro Jaycees if the Edinburgh code of golf hadn't been written. And at the same time, over at Prestwick on the West Coast, they like to say that the R&A wouldn't have anything to do but run the St. Andrews city championship if Prestwick's members hadn't decided to invent the Open championship and stage it the first twelve years of its existence. The Open championship, of course, is what we call the British Open today.

All I know is, every time somebody at Muirfield or Prestwick or Troon or Carnoustie goes out and finds an old track iron which had to have been made over two hundred years ago, somebody from the R&A will reach down into Hell Bunker or the Swilken Burn and find a club that is older. One envisions the old club makers around St. Andrews carving and hammering away these days, making an antique putter dated 1742.

What truly matters, of course, is that the whole scene is old—the gray clubhouses and the rolling land, the

Minute Books and the scrolls, the wind, and rain, and heather, the dunes and swales, everything that makes Scottish golf what it is. It had been said by many that a golfer hasn't played the game until he has gone back where it all was, and where it all is.

It is a special feeling, I think, that calls the golfer back to Scotland as the sailor is called by the sea. Take me to the grave of Old Tom Morris, a voice says. Drive me around the Road Hole. Show me where theWee Icemon chipped it in at Carnoustie. Lead me down the long, narrow eleventh at Troon where Arnie made the threes. Let me hear the groan of the Spitfire ghosts at Turnberry. Carry me over the Sleepers at Prestwick. Bend me around the archery field at Muirfield. Drown me in all of these treasures of time once more in this, still another life.

The Scots themselves relish all of this more than anyone. It is in their faces as deeply as it is in their poems. They are constantly writing poems about their bunkers, and burns and braes. "The swallows are high in an empty sky, so let's to the tee once more." That kind of thing. Or "There's none—I'll back the assertion with a wager—can play the heavy iron like the Major!" It has been estimated that more golf poetry exists in Scotland than heather.

"So let's to the tee once more," I said to the customs official at Prestwick, having de-boarded my flight from JFK. "The nature of my visit? Well, to receive a welcome and a blessing from the game. Actually, I have a meeting scheduled with Heather, Whin, Bracken & Broom, Incorporated, one of your very successful brokerage firms."

There was this tour that Keith Mackenzie, then the secretary of the R&A, had worked out. Fly to Prestwick,

the old World War II air base where everybody played
12 O'clock High, and motor from there down the West
Coast to Turnberry, the Pebble Beach of Scotland. Stay
at the Turnberry Hotel, which is the only thing there,
and covers a whole hillside, overlooking the Turnberry
course and the old RAF runways. From Turnberry, he
said, one could reach two other very famous Scottish
links—Troon and Prestwick—simply by driving once a
day over the Electric Brae, a road which goes up when
it appears to be going down. Cover the West Coast first,
said Mackenzie, then move to the Old Course Hotel at
St. Andrews where you can play the Old Course, right
outside your window, and journey north toward Dun-
dee and Carnoustie, or south toward Edinburgh and
Muirfield.

"This is the best possible route for an American,"
said Mackenzie.

"But I'm Scottish," I said. "I'm just retracing my steps
from a few hundred years before."

"Of course, dear chap," Keith said. "We're all Scottish
when it comes to golf."

He said, "Turnberry is pitched right there on the
Firth of Clyde. Tees practically hanging on the water
like Pebble. And Prestwick with those slender fairways
and blind shots, and seven bloody five pars. Too out-
dated for the Open championship, of course, but, mind
you, the Pine Valley of Scotland in a way. And wonderful
Old Troon. The 'postage stamp' green. The very first
sharp-angled dogleg. I say, Arnie argued a good case
there, didn't he?"

"Aye," I said.

"Then to the East Coast, my view," Keith said. "You'll
quarter in the Old Course Hotel, naturally, right where
the railway sheds were on the Road Hole. Walk out on

your terrace and spit in the Principal's Nose, by Jove. With the new bridge, you can reach Carnoustie in an hour now. Good old somber Carnoustie, the Barry Burn and all that. And then, of coure, there's Muirfield. Marvelous place, Muirfield. Not a burn on it, you see. Just one hundred sixty-five bunkers. You'll see a bit of sand there, I daresay."

"Aye," I said.

"Best of luck," he said. "See you at St. Andrews when you arrive. We'll have a bit of port. It goes well in the Big Room."

For some evil reason, some death wish that perhaps is concealed within us all, the first thing a touring golfer is captivated by in Scotland is the plant life adjacent to all fairways. The heather, whin, bracken, and broom. Turnberry, my first stop, had all of these other landmarks to dwell upon—holes hanging on the Firth of Clyde, as Mackenzie said, the pockmarked warplane runways now bordered by wildflowers, a bird sanctuary on an island off in the distance, the huge hotel on the hill where "God Save the Queen" reverberated from the orchestra pit in the ballroom at night through all of the tea rooms, and an RAF monument at the twelfth green commemorating those men from Turnberry's aerial fighting and gunnery school who perished, their name liveth forever with the group captain in the sky. But I was preoccupied with the rough.

You find yourself having this running commentary with your caddie, as if he's a botanist in his checkered James Cagney cap, his coat and tie, and a scruffy face which hasn't been shaved since the last air raid. His name is Jimmy or Peter or Ginger or Tip or Cecil, and chances are he caddied for Hagen at Hoylake in 1924.

"What am I in here?" I asked the one at Turnberry on the very first hole. "Is this gorse?"

"Not likely," he said. "I think that's a bush."

Your caddie is a warm, friendly man who knows his golf. You swing once and he knows your distances. If he says the shot is "a wee seven," you'd better hit it wee-ly, or a dozen of you with machetes won't be able to find the ball behind the green.

Such a hole was the fourth at Turnberry, which bears the name Woe-be-Tide. It is a 170-yard one-shotter. You practically stand on the Firth and hit into a crosswind to a green about as big as your golf bag with more water on the left and hounds of the Baskervilles on your right.

"What am I in now?" I asked, having hit a Firthlock safely to the right. "Is this heather?"

"That," he said, "is gorse. You ca'na swing softly, sir and be way o' the gorse."

"Gorse is whin, right?"

He said, "Aye, the whins we call it. You ca'na plant the whin and neither will the whin die. The whin is just here, where it always was."

I took a forceful swing with a sand iron, moving the ball about one foot, and said, "Don't forget to show me the heather when we find some."

"Aye," he said. "That's heather you're in now."

You can't often find the ball in heather. It is a stubby dwarf plant, all matted and wiry, brown at times, purple at others. You can top a shot with a driver and, whereas in America the ball is likely to run for a hundred or so yards, if in Scotland it finds a cluster of heather only a few yards away, it will go flimp—and either disappear forever, or bound straight back at you.

I could see at least half of the ball there in the heather, and I took a full swipe at it with the wedge, so hard that the caddie counted all of the cleats in my shoes and the veins in my legs, and the noise I made sounded like the Stukas had returned to drop another load on the docks at Glasgow.

And the ball didn't move at all.

"When does my hand stop tingling?" I said.

Turnberry has one hole that is more magnificent than all of the others. It is the ninth, a 425-yard hole with a tee sitting back on a ledge of jagged rock, with rocks and water bordering it on the left where a lighthouse marks the farthest point of the course from the hotel. Off to the right, beyond the plant life, is part of the old asphalt RAF runway. Behind the green is broom—whin without thorns—and little dabs of bracken, which the cows won't eat.

One finds in Scotland, however, that if the botany doesn't confuse you, the scorekeeping will. I drove well at the ninth, which means safely onto the close-cropped fescue grass which comprises all Scottish fairways. I reached the small green with one of my rare unshanked four-irons, and I stole a putt of about twenty feet for a three. Then the trouble began.

"Is this a par-four hole?" I asked the caddie.

"No, sir," he said. "It plays to a bogey five."

"Then I made an eagle," I said.

"It ca'na be an eagle, sir," he said.

"Well, what's par for the course?"

He said, "Bogey today is about seventy-six."

"But level fours is seventy-two," I said. "Shouldn't that be what I would call par?"

He thought a minute and said, "I reckon par to be about seventy-four today."

"What was it yesterday, for instance?" I asked.

"Oh, in that wind yesterday, par must have been seventy-seven or so."

I said, "Well, I think I just made an eagle."

"You did'na make an eagle, sir," he said.

"A birdie?"

"Not exactly a birdie with the helpin' wind, sir."

"A par?"

"Oh, much better than a par, it was," he said.

"So what the hell was it?"

He said, "It was a very good score, sir. Your first of the round."

There is much to see in the neighborhood of Turnberry, and along the route to either Prestwick or Troon, like a castle here and there, or a birthplace of Robert Burns, of which there must be a dozen, but never should a visitor miss that hill—that thing—called the Electric Brae. Years ago, bicyclists discovered it, one learns. They found themselves forced to pedal sweatily to get uphill when it obviously looked as if the road were going downward into the woods. It is an optical illusion, and you would lose your wallet betting on it. The proof is this: stop the car at a point where you are certain you are headed uphill. Put a golf ball on the road. It will roll uphill, that's all.

As mysterious as the Electric Brae is, it is no more mysterious than the course at Prestwick, the course where all of those early British Opens were staged beginning in 1860. Your first impression as you gaze out on a wasteland surrounded by an old stone fence is that this has to be the biggest practical joke in all of golf. I've got it, you say. You pay your green fee, put down a ball, and aim at the world, take four or five steps and are never heard from again.

Consider the first hole, only 339 yards. On your right, the stone fence, about ten feet away, separating you from a train that will come chugging by at intervals. On your left: mounds of heather and whin. Directly in front: waste. Sheer waste. Small and large clumps of it, sheltered by thin layers of fog. And the caddie hands you a driver. The fairway, presuming one is actually there, can't be more than twenty yards wide, but the caddie hands you a driver.

"*Where* is it?" I asked.

"Straightaway, sir," said Charles, who was distinguished from my caddie at Turnberry by two things. Charles wore a muffler and had his own cigarettes. "It's just there," he said. "Just to the left of the cemetery."

It is asking a lot, I know, to expect anyone to believe that you can bust a drive about 250 yards on a 339-yard hole, have a good lie in the fairway, and still not be able to see a green anywhere, but this is Prestwick.

The green was there, all right, as are all of the greens at Prestwick, but you never see them until you are on them, which is usually eight or ten strokes after leaving the tee. They sit behind little hills, or the terrain simply sinks ten or fifteen feet straight down to a mowed surface or they are snuggled over behind tall wood fences over which you have nothing to aim at but a distant church steeple.

You would like to gather up several holes from Prestwick and mail them to your top ten enemies. I guess my all-time favorite love-hate golf hole must be the third hole on this course. Like most of the holes at Prestwick, it is unchanged from the day in 1860 when Willie Park, Sr., shot 174 to become the first Open champion.

First of all, without a caddie, it would take you a week and a half to find the third tee. It is a little patch of ground roughly three yards wide perched atop a stream, a burn, rather, with the cemetery to your back and nothing up ahead except fine mist. Well, dimly in the distance, you can see a rising dune with a fence crawling across it—"the Sleepers," the caddie says. But nothing more. Nothing.

"I'll be frank, Charles," I said. "I have no idea which way to go, or what with."

"Have a go with the spoon, sir," he said.

"The *spoon*?" I shrieked. "Where the hell am I going with a spoon?"

"A spoon'll get you across the burn, sir, but it'll na get you to the Sleepers," he said.

"Hold it," I said. "Just wait a minute." My body was sort of slumped over, and I was holding the bridge of my nose with my thumb and forefinger. "These, uh, Sleepers. They're out there somewhere?"

"Aye, the Sleepers," he said.

"And, uh, they just kind of hang around, right?"

"Aye," he said. "The Sleepers have took many a golfer."

Somehow, I kept the 3-wood in play and when I reached the ball, Charles casually handed me the 4-wood. I took the club and addressed the ball, hoping to hit quickly and get on past the Sleepers, wherever they were. But Charles stopped me.

"Not that way, sir," he said.

"This *is* the way I was headed when we left the tee," I said.

"We go a bit right here, sir," he said. "The Sleepers is there just below the old fence. You want to go over the Sleepers and over the fence as well, but na too far right because of the burn. Just a nice stroke, sir, with the 4-wood."

Happily, I got the shot up and in the general direction Charles ordered, and walking toward the flight of the ball, I finally came to the Sleepers. They were a series of bunkers about as deep as the Grand Canyon. A driver off the tee would have found them, and so would any kind of second shot that didn't get up high enough to clear the fence on the dune. A worn path led through the Sleepers, and then some ancient wooden steps led up the hill and around the fence to what was supposed to be more fairway on the other side.

It wasn't a fairway at all. It was a group of grass moguls going off into infinity. It looked like a carefully arranged assortment of tiny green Astrodomes. When Charles handed me the pitching wedge, I almost hit him with it because there was no green in sight.

I got the wedge onto the green that was, sure enough, nestled down in one of those dips, and two-putted for a five that I figured wasn't a par just because the hole was 505 yards long. Charles said I had played the hole perfectly, thanks to him, and that I could play it a thousand times and probably never play it as well.

I said, "Charles, do you know what this hole would be called in America?"

"Sir?" he said.

"This is one of those holes where your suitcase flies open and you don't know what's liable to come out," I said.

"Aye, 'tis that," he said.

"One bad shot and you're SOL on this matter," I said.

"Sir?" said Charles.

"Shit out of luck," I said.

"Aye," said Charles. "At Prestwick, we call it the Sleepers."

———

Prestwick has a number of other charming atrocities. There is a 201-yard fifth hole which the caddies call the "Himalayas" which one plays with anything from a 5-iron to a driver, depending on the wind. You flog the shot over a mountainous dune and discover, on the other side, about a hundred feet down, a green. You ring a bell when you've putted out. There is a wonderful fifteenth hole of only 329 yards, straightaway, but the fairway is total heather except for the width of an umbrella, and there is no green at all that I could find. All in all, I would say that Prestwick is the most unique course in the world. There are eighteen holes but I dare any visitor to find more than, say, twelve fairways and seven or eight greens.

Only a couple of graveyards and trash piles away from Prestwick lies Troon. In fact, from the tenth tee at Prestwick you can see Troon better than you can see Prestwick. The course is on the Firth, not so much as Turnberry but more so than Prestwick, and the town is filled with small resort hotels and rooming houses which advertise bed-and-breakfast. Troon is the seaside getaway on weekends for the inhabitants of Glasgow. You can fish there, and hike, and go camping in the drizzle. But the best thing you can do if you are privileged enough is play Old Troon, the championship course of the snootiest club on the West Coast. The sektry will arrange the round if he approves of the cut of your blazer.

For the full haul of eighteen holes, Troon is not all that memorable. The rough, for one thing, is more like rugged American rough; you *can* escape from it in one hearty swing if the waist of your trousers is cinched up. Troon, I found, is what you would call a pleasant course and somehow more modern than most Scottish courses if any layout without the hint of a tree can look modern to an American.

This is not to say that Troon is devoid of character. It has several holes, as a matter of fact, which are as good as any to be found, including one of the hardest holes I have ever seen—the eleventh—not to forget two others which have been architectural landmarks since they were constructed.

The eighth, for example. This is the famed "postage stamp." It is so named because the green, which clings to nothing but the lower half of a heather-covered mound, is not much larger than a stamp. The hole measures only 125 yards, but it can play up to a 4-iron if the wind is whipping out of the north.

It did not harm the fame of the "postage stamp" that in 1923, when Troon was first used to stage the Open championship, none other than Walter Hagen made a double bogey five there to blow the title by a stroke to a Mr. Arthur Havers.

All over Scotland one continually finds par-4 holes where, at one time or another, according to the caddies, Jack Nicklaus was on in one. The hole before the "postage stamp," Troon's seventh, is such a hole. It is renowned for two other reasons; first, it is supposed to be one of the original doglegs, since the fairway curves sharply to the right, and it is also considered one of the most beautiful holes.

With the tee up on a bluff furnishing a wide view of the sea, and with the wind usually helping, you can envision how Nicklaus might have driven it those 385 yards. He caught one just right and strung it out over the sandhills, hit a downslope, and burned a path through the whin up to the putting surface.

It might well have been this good fortune back in

1962 that encouraged Jack to take out the driver at Troon's eleventh the day he had to sink a 50-foot putt for a ten. The eleventh hole is 485 yards of railroad track on the right and clusters of whin on the left. The fairway is nothing but moguls all the way with the tiny green hard by another of those old stone fences. This is the hole Palmer won that Open on, for he played it with two threes, a four and five—five under—by using a 1-iron off the tee and 2-iron to the green.

Troon makes no claim to being among the oldest clubs in Scotland—it was only built in 1878—but like any other self-respecting private domain, it has a set of relics that are said to be the oldest in Britain. The club secretary proudly pointed to a trophy case and said those clubs were found in a cupboard wrapped in a newspaper dated 1741.

"I think old Laurie over at St. Andrews is getting ready to make a set that's dated 1740," I said, being witty.

The club secretary didn't laugh.

The crass American wouldn't think much of a clubhouse at a Scottish links. There are no tennis courts, no swimming pool, and no mixed foursome room. The clubhouse is basically for the ex-wing commanders, ex-squadron leaders, and ex-group captains to have lunch in, freshen up after the daily round, and discuss the latest follies of parliament as reported by the *Daily Telegraph.* If there is a shower stall down some creaking corridor, the water is chilled and hits you with all the force of a leak in the roof. On the walls of the dining room and reading room, both of which invariably provide a sprawling view of the eighteenth green, will be oil portraits of a lot of gentlemen who look as if they might have enjoyed "taking a strap to the Wonkies," or introducing the Hun to "a bit of cold steel."

If you are as poor at geography as I am, you have to divide Scotland like this: The West Coast, where Troon, Prestwick, and Turnberry are located, is the Ireland side. At least that's what I call it. Northern Ireland sits right over there, though a fairly long carry from a beach at Turnberry. Where I was now headed was to the East Coast, the Edinburgh side as opposed to the Glasgow side, to the North Sea, to the posh area of the country where you can find St. Andrews, Muirfield, and lesser-known courses that are just as satisfying and just as haunting as any of the brand names—courses such as North Berwick (East and West), Dunbar, and Gullane No. 3, among others.

To the east is also Carnoustie, which might be my favorite Scottish word. All at the same time, it sounds like a castle you should see, something you might want to wear to a reunion of the old regiment, or something you might want to eat—"I'll just have the carnoustie with a small green salad."

What it is, of course, is maybe the toughest course in Scotland. It is long, windy, and wet. It is also smoky, dreary, and somber. Every hole starts out like the one you've just played—unreachable.

Carnoustie begins to develop a distinction around the fifth hole, I think. But maybe I felt this because my caddie had me primed. Here was the hole where the Wee Icemon, Ben Hogan, had chipped in for a birdie three in 1953 during the last round. It was where he had made the stroke, from the lower-left bunker, that launched him toward the British Open title the one and only time he ever played in it.

"He stood right here," said Philip, the caddie. "Aye, it was only a short flick of the wrist."

The sixth, too, had character, most of it provided by an electrical fence down the left-hand side of the fairway. Periodically, a sign in red letters hung on the fence which said: DO NOT TOUCH ANYTHING. IT MAY EXPLODE AND KILL YOU. On the other side of the wire, as you might guess, was a firing range used by the Ministry of Defense. The hole is 565 yards long, and the Scots named it Hogan's Alley in '53, for Ben birdied it the last two rounds.

Philip stopped at a point far beyond my tee shot down the fairway. "Here," he said, digging his shoe into the turf. "And here." He moved it a couple of inches. "Then here." He moved it another inch. "And over here." He moved his shoe about a foot.

"That's where the Icemon drove it," he said.

From here until near the finish Carnoustie became something of a blur. The wind wouldn't give my 4-wood a rest, and the steady drizzle turned my under and over cashmeres into about seven hundred pounds of inconvenient weight. The most fascinating landmark near the course, after the firing range, was Anderson Cranes and Stone-Cutting Machinery.

"Philip," I said. "Did anyone ever suggest to you that Carnoustie is *not* Antibes?"

Somewhere near the end, I vaguely recall, there is a Barry Burn that you have to cross about thirty times on the last three holes. With dry grips, maybe less.

As it turned out, I finished with a flourish. Good driver, good spoon, good 8-iron, four feet from the cup. Of course, in my haste to have Philip show me the spot where Hogan used to go to wring out his sweaters, I blew the putt. And with a number of people staring at me through the clubhouse window, too.

Later on, I was safely indoors trying to dry off and get one of those wonderful hot beers when a tall Britisher in a coat with a crest approached me.

"I say, you're the chap who was out there on the eighteenth a while ago," he said.

"Afraid so," I said.

"Bit dodgy that putt," he said. "Breaks left."

"Sure does," I said.

"Good for me, though," he said. "Took four shillings off a bloke at the bar."

Yeah, I thought, well, Hogan won the Open here and he's from my town, and Lend-Lease and—ah, screw it.

Muirfield from St. Andrews is in precisely the opposite direction of Carnoustie, and it is everything Carnoustie isn't. Muirfield is elegance and class, charm and dignity, convenience and pleasure. There is not a true distance on it, nor a fixed par, nor a name for a hole, but it is a course with a championship quality in the purest sence. There is not a tree or a bush or a burn, but there are about 4,135 bunkers and they are trouble enough. It is the only course in Scotland that takes advantage and disadvantage of the full cycle of the wind, for the outgoing nine goes clockwise and back to the clubhouse, and the back nine runs counterclockwise and returns. Par is probably 72, but it is easy to envision days when the winds would make it 76.

Muirfield is on the Firth of Forth between Gullane and North Berwick, not painfully far from Edinburgh. It is on a fine shore surrounded by estates, and one gets the idea that this area is to Edinburgh what the Hamptons are to New York City. Muirfield's clubhouse is noted for its spaciousness in comparison with other Scottish clubhouses.

Directly next door to the huge stone clubhouse with its sprawling veranda and putting green is the Greywalls Hotel, where a person might stay if he liked having a meal that only costs $6,413. Greywalls fronts on the ninth green, and the Scots have long felt that part of the vast charm of Muirfield is that a fellow can stop after nine holes and grab a tap at Greywalls—the way Americans do at their courses.

The real charm of Muirfield is in its amazing fairness and its splendid pacing, both of which are much on the order of Merion, that gem of a battleground on Philadelphia's Main Line where every club comes out of the bag every time you play it. Muirfield has short fives and long fives, short, bending fours, and long, narrow fours, short, tricky threes, and long but reachable threes. Its fairways are skinny but the lies are perfect, and there are shortcuts to be taken by the brave or long-hitting who wish to flirt with more bunkers than the eye can count.

The highest compliment anyone could pay Muirfield, I suppose, would be to say that it is a Hogan type of course. Distances are meaningless because of the wind, and Hogan always said they were meaningless, anyhow. Every shot has a look to it, he said, a certain feel. "I might hit a two-iron a hundred fifty yards," he often said.

I played Muirfield that way. My 2-irons went exactly 150 yards, and frequently off the shank of the club to the right.

"This is the course," my caddie said. "This is the best of the lot."

"I'd like to see it sometime," I said.

There are a number of spectacular holes at Muirfield, but the sixth is perhaps its finest. It is a par 4—sometimes a par 5—of 475 yards or thereabouts, an uphill-downhill dogleg left which curls around a battered rock wall which separates the course from an archery field. The landing area for the tee shot is no more than twenty yards across, and deep bunkers patrol it. With a career drive you can then get close to home with a career 3-wood to a rolling green, again framed by bunkers.

"What a hole," I said to the caddie as I stood there considering the 3-wood.

"Have a good go with a spoon," he said. "But a word of caution, sir. A ball played into Archerfield Wood is irrecoverable."

The mystique of Muirfield lingers on. So does the memory of Carnoustie's foreboding. So does the scenic wonder of Turnberry, and the haunting incredibility of Prestwick, and the pleasant deception of Troon. But put them all together and St. Andrews can play their low ball for atmosphere.

To begin with, St. Andrews is an old university town. Spires rise up over narrow streets littered with shops and cozy pubs. Students wearing red cloaks are bicycling around. Statues confront the stroller. An inn is here and there, and the North Sea just beyond.

There are four golf courses at St. Andrews: Old, New, Eton, and Jubilee, and they are all available to the public. The *new* course is over a hundred years old. Try that on for nostalgia. But no one, of course, is ever concerned about anything but the Old. The Old Course *is* St. Andrews, the R&A, all of those famed hazards. It is Jones, Vardon, Hagen, and old and young Tom Morris, and an R&A member standing on the balcony of his office in the R&A building just above the first tee surveying the entirety of the layout through a pair of mounted German submarine binoculars.

I was fortunate enough to secure lodging in the Old Course Hotel. Thus, I could walk out on my terrace and it was all there directly below me. To my left, the course stretching out to the eleventh green, and to my right, a matchless view of the eighteenth fairway leading up through the Valley of Sin with Rusacks Hotel standing there as it is supposed to be, and with the great gray edifice of the Royal & Ancient clubhouse forming a backdrop.

The Old Course has been called a lot of things because, at first glance, it looks like nothing more than a flat green city park. Some Americans have labeled it a "third-rate municipal course," and a "football field," but Bob Jones knew its subtleties better. It was, he said, the one course he would play forever if he could choose just one.

Two things strike the first-timer at St. Andrews immediately. First, the double greens. No fewer than fourteen holes share enormous putting surfaces, the second also being the sixteenth, and that sort of thing. There are two flags, naturally, and often they will be as far apart as perhaps eighty yards, with many a dip and turn between them. The erring shotmaker is apt to find the longest putts in golf at St. Andrews. Secondly, the Old Course is something of a paradise for one with a chronic hook. The first nine goes straight out, you see, with all of the heather and the sea on your right. And the back nine returns, parallel, giving the hooker all of those outgoing fairways to land on.

The difficulty of the Old Course lies in the wind and the putting, and the fantastically perfect location of such hazards as Hell Bunker, a deep and somewhat in-escapable pit at the fourteenth, the Swilken Burn, a small brook which rushes right up against the green of the first hole and catches many a soft 9-iron, and the Valley of Sin, the cavernous lower level of the eighteenth green from which three-putts and even four-putts are commonplace.

I attacked the Old Course in the company a caddie named Ginger who had merely been caddying there for forty-five years. For a few holes, he thought he had Henry Cotton again. The wind was behind and my shank, my top, my slice, and my putting jerk seemed to have disappeared. Through the tenth, I was only one over par, and I said to Ginger, "I don't know, but I think I'm bringing the Old Course to its knees."

And Ginger said, "Aye, ya made a putt or two, sir. But now we go home into the wind."

In rapid order, I was lost in the Elysian Fields, lost in the Beardies, trapped in Hell Bunker, gouged in the Principal's Nose, over the fence, smothered in heather, and even out of bounds on an overhang of the Old Course Hotel at the Road Hole. Finally, I limped up the eighteenth fairway en route to the Valley of Sin. Par for 86.

"You had a wee bit of hard luck," Ginger said. "But it can't spoil the fact that as we cum up the eighteenth, we sense a wee bit of tradition, don't we?"

The R&A member peered down from his balcony as I walked onto the green. I putted out. One final insult: a straight-in 4-footer which broke six inches. The secre-tary motioned me up for lunch in the R&A dining room. I toured the club and reread the letter that Isaac Grainger, then the president of the USGA, had written to the R&A on the occasion of its 200th birthday.

He had said, in part, "What golf has of honor, what it has of justice, of fair play, of good fellowship and sportsmanship—in a word, what is best in golf—is almost surely traceable to the inspiration of the Royal and Ancient."

I thought of those words again as I strolled back outside to stand and look at the sea, and at the town, and all across the gentle green sweep of the Old Course—the oldest course.

I had been there forever.

Afterword

I HAVE THIS NOTION that if Michael Jackson had ever taken up golf, he would never have felt the need to have lunch with orangutans—or even with Elizabeth Taylor.

Take another rich eccentric, Howard Hughes. Hughes should never have quit golf—he was once an excellent player, they say. If Hughes had stayed out there whapping it around Bel-Air, he might not have wound up wearing Kleenex boxes for house slippers and watching *Ice Station Zebra* two thousand times.

History shows us that mental problems often afflict the notoriously rich and savagely famous. Goofy things seem to happen to their heads when they are handed all those billions so quickly for doing so little.

A writer in a London newspaper said it best not too long ago, pointing out that the problems of the rich and famous are frequently *fiscal*, not mental.

Golf can do things to the head, too, of course. Yeah, you can become a different kind of nut. But at least you'll be a healthier nut mentally—and you might even be found in sensible footwear around the house.

I think one of the nicest things I can say about golf, after hanging around the game for so many years, is that it can actually save lives.

With my very own eyes, I have watched golf cure drug addiction in people. I have watched golf cure the thirst for alcohol in people. I have watched golf help people get through career setbacks. I have watched golf see people through stormy relationships and messy divorces of the male-female variety.

The importance that golf can take on in a household is both a curious and an amazing thing.

Somehow, when Martha tells Fred she wants him to clean out the garage today, this works:

"Good God, woman, don't you realize I'm supposed to be on the tee at nine thirty-seven this morning with Casey, Jerry, and Wally?"

It works, you see, because golf is *healthy.*

Which is why, when Martha tells Fred they need to go to the mall today to look at light fixtures, this doesn't work:

"Good God, woman, don't you realize I have to shoot up some heroin and drink a quart of vodka today?"

I might add that I have also watched golf lure people into the game who had never given it a thought. Not if there was a guitar handy, or a movie to produce, or a tooth to pull, or a house to build, or some tax work to be done, or a city street to jog on.

All this says something about how much the game has grown in the years I've been on this planet, or putting green, or both.

Frankly, it doesn't seem like all that long ago that my old hometown of Fort Worth only had three country clubs—Colonial, River Crest, and Glen Garden, the last being the place where Hogan and Nelson caddied as kids.

Now there are at least five others that I can name, and surely a few I don't even know about in the county, and yet I notice quite happily when I go back to visit that I can still drive anywhere I care to go around town in the same old ten minutes.

The fact is, this sort of thing has happened in virtually every city of any size over the past thirty years.

But not just in every city.

As the journalism habit keeps me traveling around, I find that I can no longer gaze at a swamp, mountainside, desert, gulch, prairie, or river bottom without seeing a golf course sitting on it.

To go along with the old-line money clubs, which got there first, this land of ours now has hotel courses, resort courses, real estate development courses, quarry courses, island-green courses, "executive" courses, replica courses, public-private courses, and lighted courses. And I suppose that somewhere there's a virtual reality country club for computer hackers who like to play Pebble Beach without leaving the lab.

All this has come about in order to accommodate the growing number of golfers, which has swollen from five million to twenty-five million while I either had my back turned or was taking a free drop from a ditch.

Of course, there are *not* twenty-five million golfers in this country who play once a week. Not yet, at least. On the other hand, it can seem like twenty-five million, or more, on those days when the groups in front of you are so agonizingly slow, thanks to watching all the Greg Normans on TV, that it may often require five or six hours to finish eighteen holes.

I don't do that anymore, by the way. When it gets that slow, I do a Daytona thing in the cart and take it to the cabin, even if I have a career round going, even if it costs me the bets I've made. It's not worth an angioplasty to watch the guy in front of me plumb-bob his way to a thrilling 96.

Along with this remarkable increase in the golfing population has come the advancement in technology—the hot ball, the nuclear shaft, the oversized club head. These inventions permit the scrawniest little orphan at my club to outhit me by 50 yards off the tee, and they permit the most awkward-looking brute to outhit me by 100 yards off the tee, and this says nothing about the 200-yard 7-irons they can both hit.

But it's okay. They love golf too, and none that I know of have taken to having lunch with orangutans.

There *is* one danger that has gone along with the game's explosion. Best to describe it by telling you about a friend of mine.

He has been arguing for the past several years that a quiet revolution has occurred and there is now a subculture in America. It's called golf, he believes. My friend obviously suffers from a disease that can only be identified as Golf Dependency, and what it has done lately is make him change his entire life.

He has gone so far as to quit his high-salaried job in the real world, and he has no prospects for any income in the foreseeable future, apart from perhaps retrieving grocery carts from supermarket parking lots.

But he is happier than I have seen him in years. And when you ask him if he's been playing any golf lately, his answer is always the same.

"Just days," he says.